• • • **Trainee Book**

The CELTA

Certificate in English Language Teaching to Adults

Course

Scott Thornbury

Peter Watkins

Published in collaboration with Cambridge ESOL

UNIVERSITY *of* CAMBRIDGE
ESOL Examinations

English for Speakers of Other Languages

CAMBRIDGE
UNIVERSITY PRESS

CAMBRIDGE UNIVERSITY PRESS
Cambridge, New York, Melbourne, Madrid, Cape Town,
Singapore, São Paulo, Delhi, Tokyo, Mexico City

Cambridge University Press
The Edinburgh Building, Cambridge CB2 8RU, UK

www.cambridge.org
Information on this title: www.cambridge.org/9780521692069

First published 2007
5th printing 2011

Printed in the United Kingdom at the University Press, Cambridge

A catalogue record for this publication is available from the British Library

ISBN 978-0-521-69206-9 Trainee Book
ISBN 978-0-521-69207-6 Trainer's Manual

Contents

Introduction

What is CELTA?

CELTA stands for the Certificate in English Language Teaching to Adults. CELTA is an initial qualification for people with little or no previous teaching experience, and is awarded by Cambridge ESOL, part of the University of Cambridge.

Candidates can take CELTA full time (typically four to five weeks), or part time (from a few months to over a year). There are five main units of learning:

- learners and teachers, and the teaching and learning context
- language analysis and awareness
- language skills: reading, listening, speaking and writing
- planning and resources for different contexts
- developing teaching skills and professionalism

Candidates are assessed throughout the course, with no final examination. An external assessor, appointed by Cambridge ESOL, moderates each course. There are two components of assessment:

- Teaching practice: candidates teach for a total of six hours, working with classes at at least two levels of ability. Assessment is based on the candidate's overall performance at the end of the six hours.
- Written assignments: candidates complete four written assignments. The assignments each focus on one of the following areas: adult learners; language systems of English; language skills; classroom teaching.

To be awarded the certificate, candidates must pass both components. There are three pass grades: *Pass*, *Pass B* and *Pass A*. A *Pass* is awarded to candidates who meet the criteria for a pass in both areas. A *Pass B* is awarded to candidates who meet the criteria for a pass in the written assignments and who demonstrate a level of achievement significantly above that required for a pass in relation to teaching practice. A *Pass A* is awarded to candidates who meet the criteria for a *Pass B* award and, in addition, demonstrate an awareness significantly higher than that required for a pass in relation to planning for effective teaching. For more information about CELTA, visit the Cambridge ESOL website: http://www.cambridgeesol.org.

What is *The CELTA Course*?

The CELTA Course is a coursebook for CELTA trainees. It is designed to be used during course input sessions (although some activities may be set in advance of sessions or as follow-up to sessions). The course consists of 40 units covering the topics on the sample CELTA course timetable (accessible on the Cambridge ESOL website), and extensive supplementary material, including advice on how to get the most out of teaching practice, a bank of classroom observation tasks, and a resource file that includes a glossary and recommendations for further reading.

The 40 units are divided into four topic areas:

- Section A: The learners and their contexts
  (Units 1 and 2) Learners' purposes, goals, expectations and learning styles
- Section B: Classroom teaching
  (Units 3–26) Presenting language, developing language skills, planning, classroom management, teaching different levels, English for special purposes, monitoring and assessing learning, choosing and using teaching resources
- Section C: Language analysis and awareness
  (Units 27–39) Grammar, vocabulary and pronunciation
- Section D: Professional development
  (Unit 40) How to get a job and continue your professional development

Each unit comprises a number of activities, starting with a warm-up and concluding with reflection. From these units and activities, course trainers will select only those elements that meet the needs and syllabus specifications of their particular courses: it is not expected that trainees will do all the units and all the activities in the book, nor that they will necessarily do the units in the order presented in the book.

The CELTA Course is not only a coursebook: it also serves as an invaluable resource for post-course review and reflection. We hope that it enriches your experience of the CELTA course, and that the CELTA course, in turn, opens the doorway to a fulfilling and worthwhile career in English language teaching.

1 Who are the learners?

A Warm-up

Answer these questions about your second-language learning experience. Then work in groups and compare your answers.

1 What was the language that you learned? Did you have a choice of language? If so, why did you choose that particular language?
2 What was your purpose for learning? Was it, for example, for travel or business, or simply curiosity? Or did you have no real purpose?
3 Did you teach yourself, have a private teacher, go to classes or study online? Or did you simply pick it up by using it?
4 If you attended classes, what were your expectations? Were they met?
5 How motivated were you? What factors either raised or lowered your motivation?
6 What level of proficiency did you hope to achieve? Did you achieve it?
7 All in all, were you satisfied with the experience? If not, what would you have done differently?

B Learners' purposes

Read these learners' profiles. Identify their reasons for learning English and answer the questions.

- Ning Wang is a Chinese Mandarin speaker who is at a further education college in Manchester, UK, doing a course as preparation for the IELTS examination, a requirement for entry into a British university.
- Lucia is a 16-year-old Italian speaker who is studying English as one of her school subjects in Bologna. She also attends an English class twice a week in a local language school.
- Kazankiran is an asylum-seeker in Canada. She speaks Kurdish and Arabic and is attending English classes with a view to settling in Canada permanently.
- Maxim (45) is of Russian origin. He lives and works in Australia and is learning English through contact with his workmates.
- Soni Kim is from South Korea. She is enrolled on an online course in order to prepare for a trip to the USA with her husband in the near future.
- Carmen, who is Brazilian, is the head of marketing in a large exporting company. She attends a one-to-one English class in São Paulo to help her in her business dealings, which are mainly with Middle Eastern clients.
- Mies is a Dutch student of economics. Nearly all of his classes at Utrecht University are conducted in English, a language he started learning when he was six.

1 What are their reasons for learning English? Use these abbreviations:
   EFL = English as a foreign language
   ESL = English as a second language
   EIL = English as an international language
   ESP = English for special (or specific) purposes
   EAP = English for academic purposes
2 Which of the above learners is probably *bilingual* in English and another language? Who is – or may one day be – *multilingual*?
3 Whose first language is likely to contribute positively to their learning of English? Whose is not? Why?
4 Who is *learning* English, as opposed to simply picking it up (or *acquiring* it)? What is the difference?
5 Who is probably getting the most *exposure* to English, and who is getting the least? Who are already *users* of English, as opposed to simply *learners*?
6 Who is likely to be the most motivated? Who the least?
7 Which of the above learners (if any) most closely fits the profile of the kind of learner you are expecting to teach, and the kind of situation you are expecting to teach in?

C Learners' goals

1 Match these statements with four of the learners in section B.

a I know I make many mistakes when I speak. But people understand me, and, look, I'm too old to learn to speak English perfectly. Maybe I would like to lose my strong accent, though.
b My dream would be to speak English like a native speaker, fluently, and with a native speaker accent, so I can forget my old life and begin a new life here.
c I just need the basics: a few useful phrases to get by, and practice in understanding people, but I don't need to read or write. Besides, I don't have much time.
d I need not only specialised English but also social English for chatting, and I need to be able to write correctly the kinds of things I do in my work.

2 Plot the four learners on this cline, depending on their language learning goals.

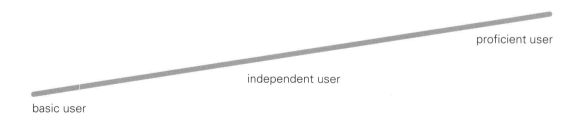

proficient user

independent user

basic user

D Learners' expectations

Read what Ning Wang and Lucia said about their English classes, and answer the questions.

1 What expectations did Ning Wang have?
2 Where did his expectations originate?
3 How realistic were his expectations?
4 Why is Lucia happier than Ning Wang with an informal, group-centred approach?
5 How appropriate are the teaching methods in each case?

Ning Wang:

'At first I was very surprised that the teacher told us we should call him by his first name, Alan. Also, we didn't sit in rows, but in a half circle. I was not happy because we didn't use the book very much, and we didn't study many grammar rules. Alan made us work in groups, but I didn't enjoy this because I was making mistakes and no one corrected them. Alan explained that it was important to speak and not to worry about making mistakes. But I do worry. I need to get a good mark in the exam.'

Lucia:

'I like my evening class because it is not as big as the class at school, and it's more fun. Sometimes we play games and listen to songs. At school we do mainly grammar exercises, and there's no chance to speak. In the evening class we have discussions in groups, or we write a story together. Another difference is that the teacher speaks to us only in English, but at school the teacher often explains things in Italian. The only bad thing in the evening class is that some of the boys misbehave and the teacher doesn't know how to control them.'

REFLECTION

1 Work in pairs. Write questions for a diagnostic interview with the learners in your teaching practice class. (If this is not possible, write questions that your trainer may be able to answer.) Find out about their *purposes*, *goals* and *expectations*, and their previous language learning experiences.
2 Hold interviews with your learners.
3 Compare your learners' responses. What are the implications for the way you teach this group?

2 Learners as individuals

A Warm-up

Work in groups. Describe two very different learners. Compare their:

* personality
* previous educational background
* motivation

What was the effect of these differences in the classroom?

B Learning style

There are a variety of ways of describing learning style. One is to imagine two intersecting axes or clines: a *studial–experiential* axis, and a *passive–active* axis, as in the following diagram:

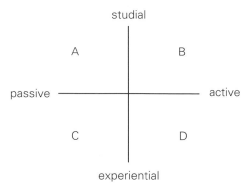

A *studial* learner is one who prefers more formal study (such as in classrooms) over learning by experience (such as through chatting with native speakers). But, at the same time, a studial learner may be either active or passive in the way they study. An *active studial* learner (Type B), for example, would be self-directed, actively working out rules from examples and capable of working alone. A *passive studial* learner (Type A), on the other hand, relies more on the teacher, likes to be told the rules, and is less confident about taking initiative.

1 Describe the characteristics of Type C and D learners. What kind of activities might they enjoy?

2 Write eight questions to use as a diagnostic test of learning style. Follow the example below.

   1 *Do you like learning and memorising rules from grammar books? (Yes = Type B learner).*

C Multiple intelligences

Another way of viewing learning style is in terms of different kinds of *intelligence*. Some intelligences that have been proposed are:

* verbal: the ability to use language in creative ways
* logical/mathematical: the ability for rational, analytic thinking

- visual: the ability to form mental models and use mental imagery
- kinesthetic: the ability to express oneself through body movement
- musical: musical and rhythmic ability
- interpersonal: the ability to understand other people's feelings and wishes
- intrapersonal: the ability to understand oneself

According to this view, the best learning opportunities are those that match the learner's most developed intelligence. Thus, learners with a strong logical/mathematical intelligence would benefit from problem-solving activities such as ones involving sorting sentences into different categories and then working out rules.

1   Read this activity and decide which intelligence it favours.

> **in class**
>
> 1 Ask for one student to volunteer to be interviewed about a topic of her choice, and ask for a volunteer interviewer.
>
> 2 Tell the group that any time anyone wants to take over as interviewer, they just go up and touch the current interviewer on the shoulder; they then take over as interviewer.
>
> Students can also replace the interviewee in the same way.
>
> A group member can do this at any time.
>
> 3 Explain that the idea is to do it in a harmonious way, so that the interview proceeds smoothly.

Multiple Intelligences in EFL Puchta and Rinvolucri

2   Suggest language learning activities that would favour these intelligences:

- visual intelligence
- kinesthetic intelligence
- musical intelligence

D   Learning strategies and learner training

1   Read what four learners say about their learning strategies, and answer the questions.

Learner A

> When I'm watching a TV programme or a film in English, I try to echo what the speakers are saying under my breath, almost at the same time they are saying it.

Learner C

> I always try to sit next to those students in class who I know like to do pairwork.

Learner B

> I write new words on to Post-it notes and I stick them on a big map of the world I have in my study. I try to make an association with the word and the place on the map.

Learner D

> When I'm reading in English and I come across a word I don't know, I try to read on a bit, to see if the meaning comes clearer.

1   What aspects of language learning (such as grammar, vocabulary, etc.) does each strategy target?
2   What learning principle does each one seem to exemplify? For example, Learner A: *repetition aids memory; production helps pronunciation.*

2 *Learner training* refers to training learners to make the most of their individual learning *style*, and to adopt effective learning *strategies*. Learner training ideas are often integrated into course book materials.

Identify the learner training purposes of these three activities.

Over to us! Palencia and Thornbury

Using a dictionary

1 Read this dictionary definition of the word *commuter* and answer the questions below.

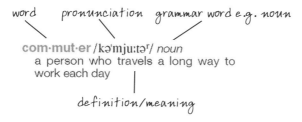

1 Who is the commuter in these sentences, Joao or Rose?
  a Joao lives in London and works in London.
  b Rose lives in Canterbury and works in London.
2 Where is the stress on the word *commuter*?
3 How is it marked in the dictionary?

2 Check the meaning and pronunciation of new words in the poem. Use a dictionary or the wordlist on page 138.

3   🔲 Listen to the poem. Is your pronunciation correct?

4 Say the poem to another student.

The Beginners' Choice Mohamed and Acklam

Learning tip *Making notes on verbs*

When you write down a new verb, make notes about it. Is it regular or irregular? How do you spell the different forms? How do you pronounce the endings?

watch (R)	watches /IZ/	watching	watched /t/
take (IR)	takes /s/	taking	took

Touchstone McCarthy, McCarten, Sandiford

3 Suggest ways to help learners make the most of the advice in the activities.

E Learner autonomy

Good learners generally take responsibility for their own learning, both inside and outside the class. That is, they take steps to become autonomous.

Advise the following learners on how to continue their language learning outside the classroom.

a

I'd like to read in English but I don't know where to start; I'm an intermediate student.

b

I don't live in an English-speaking country. Where can I get more listening practice in English – something not too difficult?

c

I like movies, but most movies in English are too difficult to understand without subtitles.

d

Is learning the words in the dictionary a good way of increasing my vocabulary? If not, what are the alternatives?

e

Our teacher doesn't give us homework, but I think I need to practise grammar. What can I do?

f

How can I use the internet to help me practise my English?

g

Where can I get speaking practice? (I don't live in an English-speaking country.)

REFLECTION

Work in groups of three. Prepare a poster or overhead transparency entitled *Dealing with classroom diversity: dos and don'ts*.

3 Foreign language lesson

A Warm-up

Work in groups of three or four. Tell your group:

- which languages you can speak
- what your first language class was like
- which picture looks most like your language classroom

a

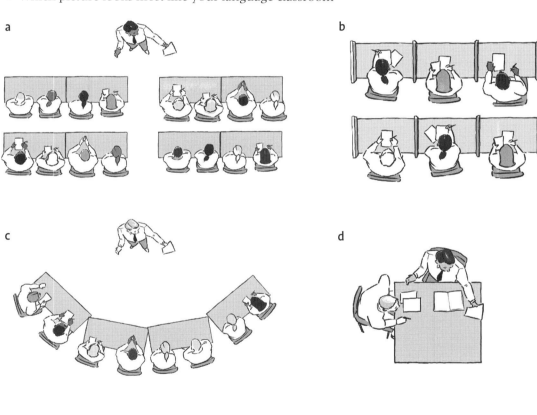

b

c

d

e

B Classroom teaching

B A foreign language lesson

A teacher will give you a short lesson in a foreign language.

C After your lesson

Work in pairs or groups of three. Try to remember as much as you can of the lesson.

1 Write down the order in which things happened in the lesson.
2 Divide what happened into stages ('chunks' of the lesson).
3 Describe how you felt during each stage of the lesson.
4 Say how the teacher:
- set up activities
- involved the learners
- made meanings clear
- presented new words or expressions
- dealt with errors

D Comparing languages

Work in pairs. Tell your partner about any differences you noticed between the language you learned and English. Think about:

- word order
- unfamiliar sounds
- the way sounds combined
- pieces of grammar or vocabulary (such as how plurals are signalled).

REFLECTION

Think about the questions. When you are ready, compare your ideas with a partner's.

1 Do you think you'll be able to remember what you learned in seven days' time?
2 What have you learned from this experience about learning a new language?
3 What have you learned from this experience about teaching a new language?

4 Classroom management

A Warm-up

Read the following statements. Do you agree or disagree? Compare your answers with a partner.

		Agree	Disagree
a	Avoid using too many gestures – they are very distracting for learners.		
b	Don't point at learners – it can seem very aggressive.		
c	Classrooms are places of study – so they should be largely quiet.		
d	If learners want to make a contribution, they should put up their hand and wait to be asked.		
e	Demonstrating activities is sometimes better than explaining activities.		

B Classroom organisation

1 Look at these diagrams and say which arrangement (1–4) would be most suitable for the classes below. Give some reasons for your choices.

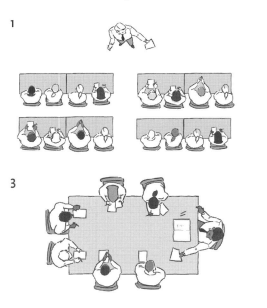

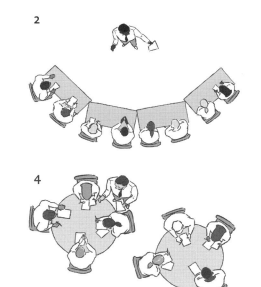

- a large class
- a small, business English class
- a grammar presentation

- pairwork
- groupwork
- a written exam

B Classroom teaching

2 Think back to the foreign language lesson (Unit 3), and answer these questions.

1 What activities did you do in pairs or groups? What was the purpose of these stages?
2 What are the benefits of pairwork and groupwork in a language classroom?
3 What are the potential drawbacks to using pairwork and groupwork?

3 Work in pairs. Say what the pictures below suggest about the best use of the whiteboard.

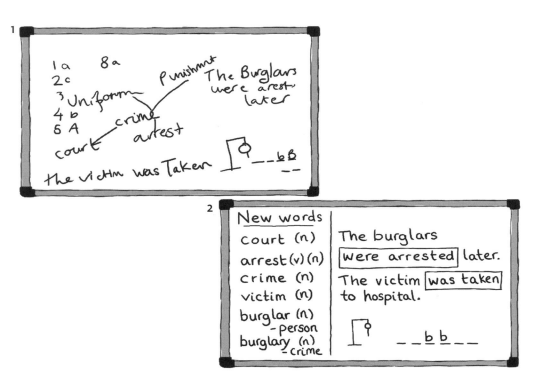

C Grading language

One of the most important things that teachers have to learn is how to adjust their language to make it appropriate for different groups of learners, particularly lower-level learners.

Read sentences a–g. Tick five sentences that offer good advice. Cross out the other two sentences. Then compare your answers with a partner.

a Pronounce each word slowly and deliberately.
b Use gestures, pictures and other things that will support what you are saying to make it easier to understand.
c Speak with natural rhythm and intonation.
d Miss out small words (articles, prepositions, auxiliary verbs and so on) so that learners can focus on the 'content' words and understand the message.
e Speak at a natural speed, but pause slightly longer after each 'chunk', if necessary.
f Try to avoid 'difficult' vocabulary (for example, very idiomatic language).
g Try to avoid complex grammar patterns.

D Giving instructions

1 Read the descriptions. Which teacher is easier to understand?

Both teachers are giving instructions for the same activity to an intermediate class.

Teacher 1:

OK, so if you wouldn't mind, open your books and look at the pictures about what the man does now and what he used to do – OK yeah, they're on page 87 – yeah you can find them in just a sec, doesn't really matter now – OK – they're just some ideas for you to think about. OK, and then what I want you to do is, you're going to write some sentences, about four, maybe a few more – don't worry if you find it difficult, just have a go anyway. So, write some sentences about things you used to do, but you don't do now. OK? And when you've done that I want you to compare them with your partner – or you can work in threes if you'd rather – I don't think it matters too much – OK, so do you understand all that? – and then I want you to mingle around and then find someone that you have something in common with. Have you got that? All right, so let's start – I would like you to write some sentences.

Teacher 2:

So look at these pictures. [Teacher holds up the book and points to the pictures.] You can use these for ideas, if you want. And then write some sentences about things you used to do, but you don't do now. Write four sentences, please.
[Learners write some sentences.]
OK, let me stop you there – don't worry if you've only written three. Now compare your sentences with a partner.
[Teacher indicates who should work with who and then learners compare.]
OK – good – now, I want you to stand up – talk to as many people as you can and find people that used to do the same things as you. OK? So, for this do you speak or write? [Learner answers 'speak'] OK, and do you speak to one person or lots of people? [*Learner answers: 'lots'*] OK, so, stand up, please.
[*Learners stand up and mingle.*]

2 Explain how Teacher 2 makes the instructions easier for the learners to understand.

* ....

* ....

* ....

* ....

* ....

E Trainees' queries

As part of the training process, trainees are asked to write an evaluation of their own lessons.

1 Read the trainees' reflective comments, and discuss possible solutions to the problems that they express.

Trainees' comments

1 I wasn't sure what to do when they were writing sentences. I knew they hadn't all finished but I didn't want the others to wait too long doing nothing.

2 I didn't enjoy it much. There were a few students who just spoke their own language the whole way through. I did say 'in English' once but it didn't do much good.

3 I wasn't sure what to do in the pairwork bit. I thought my instructions were OK, but it was obvious when they started that some of the students hadn't understood, and so I tried to go round to each group and sort it out. I think they did get it in the end.

4 The students were all doing the pairwork exercise and I just stood there. I wasn't sure what I should do really.

5 I tried to ask more learners questions today. I know I just kept asking the same people in my last lesson. But it was embarrassing. I asked Kim what she thought and it was so quiet I couldn't hear her. Even when I got really close to her it was still difficult.

6 I really wanted to use pairwork but I had an odd number, so I did the activity with one of the students. Was this right?

2 Now match the trainees' comments (1–6) with the trainer's advice (a–f).

Trainer's advice

a
You did OK here. You were there to help if they needed it, but don't interrupt if everything is going well. Just listen to what they say.

b
OK – you did well to sort the problem out, but quite a lot of time was wasted, particularly for the last pair you got to. If there's a fairly general problem, don't be afraid to stop the activity and give the instructions again.

c
Well, that learner is quiet. But if you get closer to learners they often get even quieter because they talk to you – not the class. Try getting further away and just saying something like 'a bit louder, so everyone can hear'.

d
I thought you made a pretty good decision here. You have to get the right balance. Reassure learners that they don't always have to finish – or alternatively, have something ready for the quick finishers to do.

e
If you do this it becomes very hard for you to know what the other learners are doing, or to respond if they need help or guidance. You need to think about how you will deal with awkward numbers before the lesson – usually a group of three is fine.

f
I think part of the problem was that they didn't quite understand what you wanted them to do at times. It was good that you said something but you probably needed to be a little more assertive about it – at least repeat it. You could try to move learners around a bit so that they are not always sitting next to people who speak the same language.

3   Ask your trainer any other questions you have about classroom management.

Classroom application

Think about your next teaching practice lesson.

* What will be the best seating arrangements? Will they be the same throughout the lesson?
* Plan the instructions that you will need to give.
* Will you use the board in the lesson? What will you need to write? When would it be appropriate to erase what you write?
* At what points in the lesson will you monitor the learners? What will you be looking and listening for?

REFLECTION

Work in pairs or groups of three. Write some advice about classroom management using these terms:

* seating
* pairwork
* monitor
* language grading
* giving instructions
* boardwork
* early finishers

5   Presenting vocabulary

A Warm-up

1   Choose one type of book to take to a country where you don't speak the language.

    a a dictionary   b a phrase book   c a grammar reference book

    Compare ideas with a partner. Explain your choice.

2   Work in groups of three. Read the quotation. Do you agree with Wilkins? Why?/Why not?

> 'The fact is that while without grammar very little can be conveyed, without vocabulary nothing can be conveyed.'

Linguistics in Language Teaching Wilkins

B Form, meaning and use

1   Read these entries from the *Cambridge Advanced Learner's Dictionary*. What information is given about:

    a   the form of each word
    b   the meaning of each word
    c   the use of each word?

---

euphemism /ˈjuː.fə.mɪ.zᵊm/ *noun* [C or U] a word or phrase used to avoid saying an unpleasant or offensive word: *'Senior citizen' is a euphemism for 'old person'*. ○ *The article made so much use of euphemism that often its meaning was unclear.* **euphemistic** /ˌjuː.fəˈmɪs.tɪk/ *adj* **euphemistically** /ˌjuː.fəˈmɪs.tɪ.kli/ *adv*

---

eyeball /ˈaɪ.bɔːl/ ⑤ /-bɑːl/ *verb* [T] INFORMAL to look closely at someone: *He eyeballed me across the bar.*

---

heady /ˈhed.i/ *adj* having a powerful effect, making you feel slightly drunk or excited: *a heady wine/perfume* ○ *In the heady days of their youth, they thought anything was possible.*

---

2 Discuss what it means to 'know a word'. For example, what do you need to know in order to use a word productively (in speaking or writing)?

3 What are the implications of the above for the teaching of vocabulary?

C Learning about form and meaning

Dictionaries are an effective way of learning vocabulary, particularly when learners are working outside the class, but there are many other ways that teachers can teach words and phrases.

1 Read these lesson transcripts and complete the table below.

a Beginners' class (1)
  [Teacher holds up a picture of a doctor.]
  T: Listen: doctor – doctor. Say it.
  Class: Doctor
  [Teacher holds up a picture of a nurse.]
  T: Listen: nurse – nurse. Now you. Say it for me.
  Class: Nurse.
  [Teacher writes *doctor* and *nurse* on the board.]

b Beginners' class (2)
  T: [Teacher points to the door] Look – the door is open – open. [Teacher closes the door.] Now the door is shut – shut. [Teacher opens the door.] Open. [Teacher closes the door.] Shut. Now you. Say it.
  S1:   Open.
  T: No – look. Shut.
  S1:   Shut.
  T: Good – everyone.
  Class: Shut.
  [Teacher opens the door.]
  T: Now.
  Class: Open.
  [Teacher writes *open* and *shut* on the board.]

c False beginners' class
  [Teacher holds up a picture of a pilot.]
  T: Do you know what job this is? What does this person do?
  S1:   In a plane.
  T: Yeah, good, he flies a plane, but what is the word for his job?
  S2:   Driver.
  T: That's good – we can say that for a car or a train, but for a plane?
  S2:   Pilot.
  T: Good – that's right – he's a pilot.
  [Teacher writes *pilot* on the board.]

d Elementary class
  S1:   What means *fruit* /friːt/?
  T: Pronunciation – /fruːt/ – like *boot* – can you say it?
  S1:   Fruit /fruːt/.
  T: Good – apples, oranges, bananas are types of fruit.
  S1:   Oh, yeah, OK – thank you.

e Intermediate class

S1:	Sorry, what does *enormous* mean?
T:	Does anyone know that word – *enormous*?
S2:	Big.
T:	Yeah, OK, just big? Or very big?
S3:	Very big.
T:	That's right – very big.

[Teacher writes *enormous* on the board]

f Advanced class

S1:	It says *flattery* here. What's that?
T:	It's when you say nice things to someone – usually because you want something from them.

	How is the meaning conveyed?	Is the spoken form practised?	How is the written form made clear?
a Beginners' class (1)	by using pictures	yes	The teacher writes it on the board.
b Beginners' class (2)			
c False beginners' class			
d Elementary class			
e Intermediate class			
f Advanced class			

2 Answer the questions.

1 As well as pictures, what other ways of illustrating the meaning of a word could a teacher use?

2 In the intermediate class (e), a learner asks a question but the teacher doesn't answer it immediately. Why not, do you think?

3 Work together. How would you teach these groups of words? You can use more than one method per group.

Group 1: a pet   to put down (a pet)   to vaccinate (intermediate class)
Group 2: to dig   to paint   to saw (pre-intermediate class)
Group 3: grape   cherry   strawberry (elementary class)
Group 4: slap   smack   punch (upper-intermediate class)

D Eliciting vocabulary

1 Work in pairs. Describe the different ways the teacher teaches the words *doctor*, *nurse* and *pilot* in section C1 (a and c). Explain why the teacher uses different strategies.

2 Read this advice for eliciting vocabulary. Which points are helpful?

a Try to trick the learners or they will find it too easy.

b Plan how you will elicit things before the lesson.

c Keep eliciting as simple and quick as possible.
d Make sure you elicit everything; never give in and just tell the learners.
e If the learners don't get the word quickly, try giving them the first sound of the word.

Compare ideas with a partner.

3 Suggest ways to elicit the following words:

a *watch* (noun)   b *game show*   c *to flatter*   d *hurricane*

E Checking understanding

1 Work in pairs. Discuss the strengths and weaknesses of these techniques for checking that learners have understood new words.

a The teacher asks a learner to translate the word (or phrase) into their own language.
b The teacher asks *Do you understand*?
c The teacher asks the students to use the word in a sentence.
d The teacher asks short, easy-to-answer questions. For example: *If you are head over heels in love, are you in love a lot, or a little bit*?

2 Work in pairs. Read the lesson transcript.

a What is the purpose of the teacher's questions?
b Complete the students' answers (1–6).
c What do you notice about the answers?

The teacher has just taught the word *shoplift*, and given the example sentence *The kids were caught shoplifting sweets*.

T:	Did the kids pay for the sweets?
Ss:	1
T:	Is this a crime?
Ss:	2
T:	Can you shoplift a washing machine?
Ss:	3
T:	Can you shoplift a watch?
Ss:	4
T:	So, is shoplifting used about very big things?
Ss:	5
T:	Can it be used about very valuable things?
Ss:	6

3 Read these questions for checking the understanding of *handbag*. Cross out the ones that aren't useful.

a What colour is this handbag?
b Do you put big things or small things in a handbag?
c Do men and women use them, generally?
d Do you like this handbag?
e Would a handbag be used every day, or just when you are travelling?

4 Read the sentences and write questions to check understanding of the bold words and phrases.

a She picked up her **briefcase** and left.
(The teacher is worried that 'briefcase' will be confused with 'suitcase'.)

b Could you **give me a hand** with the housework?
(The teacher is worried that the learners will not realise that 'give me a hand' is informal.)

c The car was **a write-off** after the accident.

d Houses are often more expensive near the **coast**.

e What have you done? Why are you **limping**?

F Practising vocabulary

Work in groups. Discuss the differences between the three practice activities (a–c) below.

1 What level is each activity suitable for?
2 Which activities could be set for homework?
3 How long would each activity take to do?
4 Which skills (reading, writing, listening or speaking) does each activity practise?

a The learners discuss transport problems and developments in their own countries.

b Learners work in small groups. The teacher gives each group a set of cards with one of the target words written on each card. One learner must take a card and can use mime, drawings, definitions, relationships with other words, or any other means to elicit the word from the other members of her group.

c The teacher prepares a gap-fill exercise and the learners have to complete the sentences with the target words and phrases. For example: An accident on a motorway often leads to long .... (answer: *traffic jams*).

G Classroom application: microteaching

Work in groups. Your trainer will give you a set of words to teach to the class.

- How will you convey the meaning of the words?
- How will you make both the written and spoken forms clear?
- How will you check that the words have been understood?

When you have prepared what you want to do, teach the words to the class.

REFLECTION

Work in groups. Think about the lesson you helped to prepare. Discuss the questions.

a Did the mini lesson proceed as you imagined?
b Was there anything about the plan that you could have improved?
c How do you think it would have been different with 'real' language learners?
d Did you learn anything from the way in which the other groups approached the task?

6 Presenting grammar (1)

A Warm-up

Answer the questions.

1 Imagine you are trying to learn a new computer program. Do you prefer:

- to be told how to do it?
- to be shown how to do it?
- to read how to do it in the manual?
- to try using it and find out for yourself?
- a combination of these?

2 Would you learn the grammar of another language following the same principles? Why/why not?

B Three presentations

Your trainer is going to present a grammar item in three different ways, and you are going to take the role of learners.

After the three mini-lessons, discuss these questions:

1 Which lesson did you prefer? Why?

2 Which word(s) sum up the approach of each lesson? Choose from the list below:

- demonstration
- personalisation
- situation
- examples
- explanation
- text

C Conveying the meaning of a grammar item

In the previous activity, your trainer used both 'live' actions and an invented situation to convey the meaning of *going to*. Other ways of conveying grammatical meaning include the use of pictures (called visual aids), and the use of texts to provide a context.

The presentation of new language using texts is dealt with in Unit 12.

B Classroom teaching

1   Look at these two pictures. What grammar structure(s) could you present, using one or both of them?

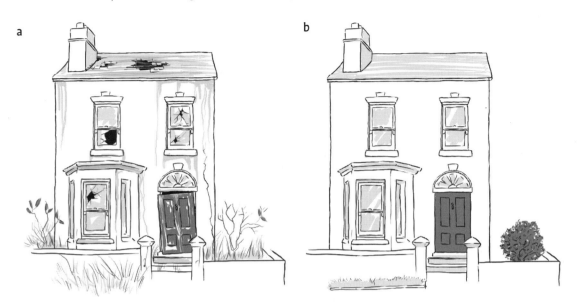

a   b

2   Work in groups. Complete the table by suggesting at least one way you could convey the meaning of each
    of the following grammar items. Give details. (*Going to* has been done for you, with three suggestions.)

Grammar item	Demonstration	Visual aids	Situation
going to (future intentions)	Point to a window in the classroom. Say 'I'm going to open the window'. Pause, and then open it. Repeat with door, etc.	Show the class some things you have, like tickets, and use these to tell them your future plans.	Draw face on board plus thought bubble. Write *cinema*, *gym*, etc. in bubble, and elicit the character's plans for the coming weekend.
can/can't (for ability)			
used to (for past habits)			
present continuous (for activities happening at the moment of speaking)			
must have done (for making deductions about past situations)			

3   Work in groups. Choose one of your presentation ideas from the above table. Plan out the steps you
    would take to convey the meaning in class.

D Highlighting the form of a new grammar item

Learners need to know both the form and meaning of new language items.

1 Read this transcript of a grammar presentation. Identify the points in the transcript where the teacher:

- conveys the meaning
- highlights the spoken form
- highlights the written form

a T: This is Elka. She went shopping yesterday. First she went to the supermarket. She bought some milk. Then she went to the greengrocer's. She bought some bananas. Then she went to the post office, and bought some stamps. Finally, she went to the newsagent's to buy a newspaper. But she couldn't find her money. (Teacher pats pockets). Where is her wallet? Where did she leave it? Did she have it in the supermarket? [Ss: Yes]. Did she have it in the greengrocer's? [Ss: Yes] Did she have it in the post office? [Ss: Yes]. Did she have it in the newsagent's? [Ss: No]. Where was the last place she had it? [Ss: In the post office.] So, where did she leave it, probably? [Ss: In the post office.] Are you sure? [Ss: Yes.] Absolutely? [Ss: Not absolutely]. So, what can we say?

b S1: She probably leave it in the post office.

c T: Listen: *She must have left it in the post office. She must have left it. Must have. Must've. She must've left it in the post office.* Everybody.

d Ss: She must've left it in the post office.

e T: Do we know for sure?

f Ss: No.

g T: Is it probable?

h Ss: Yes.

i T: So, what do we say?

j S1: She must've left it in the post office.

k T: [writes *She must have left it in the post office* on the board] She must have – must've – left it in the post office. Tell me about the grammar of *left*. What is this?

l St 2: Past tense.

m T: Not exactly. It's the past participle: *leave, left, left.* [writes *must +have* + past participle on the board].

2 Work in pairs. Discuss these questions.

1 Why do you think the teacher asks *Do we know for sure?* ? (Turn e)
2 Why does the teacher highlight the spoken form before the written form?
3 What is the teacher's purpose in asking *Tell me about the grammar of 'left'. What is this?* (Turn k)?

Checking understanding is dealt with in Unit 7.

3 Work in groups. Go back to the presentations you were planning in activity C3. Include a stage where you highlight the spoken and written forms of the new grammar item.

4 Demonstrate your presentation, using the rest of the class as learners.

REFLECTION

Look back at what you have done in this unit. Look at the following statements and complete the table. When you are ready, compare your answers with a partner. Can you add any other statements to the table?

- Involve learners in the process as much as possible.
- Check that learners have understood the meaning.
- Give a lecture about grammar.
- Always use the same presentation technique.
- Highlight the form.
- Remember that different learners may have different preferences for how new language items are presented.

Presenting new grammar items	
DOs	*DON'Ts*

7 Presenting grammar (2)

A Warm-up

Work in groups. Write at least five sentences beginning *A good grammar presentation should* ... . Compare your sentences with those of other groups. Do you agree?

B Checking understanding

1 A teacher is teaching *used to*, with *She used to live in Athens* as a model. Which of the questions a–e is a useful check of the learners' understanding of the concept?

  a Do you understand?
  b Did she use to live in Athens?
  c How do you say that in your language?
  d Did she live in Athens in the past? Does she live there now?
  e Which picture is best?

1997

now

Compare your ideas with a partner.

2 Work in pairs. Write questions to check the understanding of the structures in bold. (Assume that the learners understand the individual words.)

  a **I'm flying** to New York tomorrow (the present continuous used for a future plan/arrangement).
  b By the time I met her, she **had broken up** with Chris.
  c **If** I **was** Prime Minister, I **would give** everyone more holidays.

> Checking understanding of vocabulary using similar techniques is dealt with in Unit 5.

B Classroom teaching

C Timelines

Timelines are simple diagrams that can help some learners to see relationships between verb forms and their time reference. This diagram illustrates the sentence 'I'm reading a book at the moment'.

Notice that the line starts 'before now' and continues 'beyond now'. Here, the wavy line is usedto indicate the temporariness implied in the sentence.

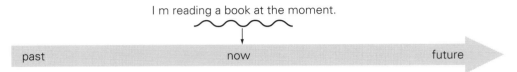

There is no one correct way to draw timelines but learners need to know the conventions you are using.

1 Work in pairs. Match the sentences (a–d) with the timelines (i–iv).

a She used to ride a motorbike.
b She used to live in Athens.
c I'm living in Australia at the moment.
d I get up at 6.30 every morning.

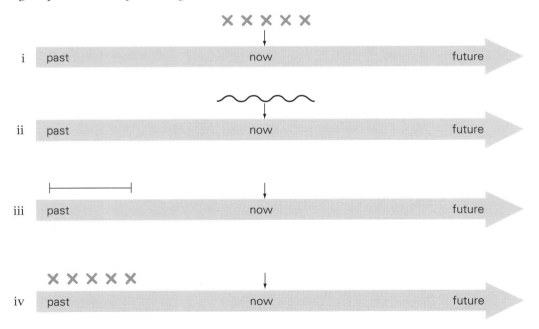

2 Draw timelines for these sentences.

e The business will have closed down by the end of the year.
f I'll still be lying on a beach when you go back to work.
g I've been working there for ages.
h By the time I met her, she had broken up with Chris.

D Ways of practising grammar

Work in groups. Compare the following four grammar practice activities. They are all part of the same lesson, contrasting *will* and *going to*.

1 In what ways are the practice activities similar and in what ways are they different?
2 In each activity, is the emphasis on practising the form, the meaning, or both?
3 What language skills (speaking, listening, reading and writing) are practised in each activity?

3 *I think I'll …*

1 Use the prompts in **A** to make sentences with *I think … will*. Match them with a sentence in **B**.

Example
I think Jeremy will win the match. He's been playing really well recently.

A
a … Jeremy/win the match
b … it/be a nice day tomorrow
c … I/pass my exams
d … you/like the film
e … we/get to the airport in time
f … you/get the job

B
☐ But we'd better get a move on.
☑ He's been playing really well recently.
☐ The forecast is warm and dry.
☐ You've got all the right qualifications.
☐ It's a lovely story, and the acting is superb.
☐ I've been revising for weeks.

2 Now make sentences with *I don't think … will* with the words from **A** in Exercise 1. Match them with a sentence in **C**.

Example
I don't think Jeremy will win the match. He hasn't practised for ages.

C
☐ There's too much traffic.
☐ I haven't done any revision at all.
☐ The forecast said rain and wind.
☑ He hasn't practised for ages.
☐ You're too young and you've got no experience.
☐ It's not really your cup of tea.

New Headway (Intermediate)
Soars and Soars

> Practising new language is dealt with more fully in Unit 8.

3 Make true sentences about *you*.

Example
I/bath tonight
I think I'll have a bath tonight/I don't think I'll have a bath tonight.

– it/rain tomorrow
– I/go shopping this afternoon
– I/be a millionaire one day
– I/eat out tonight
– we/have a white Christmas
– the teacher/give us a lot of homework

4 Grammar

Underline the correct verb form in the sentences.

Example
'Oh, dear. I'm late for work.
'Don't worry. *I'm going to give/I'll give* you a lift.'

a 'I've got a headache.'
'Have you? Wait a minute. *I'll get/I'm going to get* you an aspirin.'
b 'It's Tony's birthday next week.'
'Is it? I didn't know. *I'll send/I'm going to send* him a card.'
c 'Why are you putting on your coat?'
'Because *I'll take/I'm going to take* the dog for a walk.'
d 'Are you and Alan still going out together?'
'Oh, yes. *We'll get married/We're going to get married* next year.'
e (a telephone conversation)
'Would you like to go out for a drink tonight?'
'*I'll watch/I'm going to watch* the football on television.'
'Oh! I didn't know it was on.'
'Come and watch it with me!'
'OK. *I'll come/I'm going to come* round at about 7.30.'
f 'Did you phone Peter about tonight?'
'No, I forgot. *I'll do/I'm going to do* it now. What's his number?'

B Classroom teaching

E Planning a grammar lesson

Work in pairs. Complete the lesson plan using the boxes below.

Lesson plan
Aim: Expressing past habits with *used to* + base form.

Stage	Procedure
Building context	1
2	Teacher says 'David used to play football'.
Highlight meaning	3
4	The teacher repeats the model sentence with natural linking, stress and intonation. The class repeats.
Checking understanding	5
6	The teacher writes the model sentence on the board. Draws a box round 'used to' and writes 'base form' over 'play'.
Summarise 'rule'	7
8	Learners choose an activity they enjoyed as children and then walk round the class asking if other people used to do the same thing.
Report back	9
10	The learners discuss their memories of their first school in small groups.
Report back	The teacher asks some individuals what they talked about. Afterwards she writes some errors she heard on the board and asks learners to correct them.

a	The teacher draws a timeline on the board, showing a period in the past with several crosses within it.
b	Highlight spoken form
c	Highlight written form
d	The teacher asks some individuals how many people shared their interest and corrects errors if they are made.
e	The class talks about what things they enjoyed doing when they were children.
f	Teacher says '"used to" + infinitive can be used to talk about things we regularly did in the past, but don't do now'.
g	Freer practice
h	Model sentence
i	Restricted practice
j	Teacher asks 'Did he play football in the past?' (Yes) 'Does he play football now?' (No)

REFLECTION

Choose a grammar lesson from one of the books you are using for teaching practice. Answer the questions.

a   What stages in the presentation can you identify?
b   Is the new language contextualised?
c   Is the meaning made clear?
d   Is the form highlighted?
e   Are there any practice activities that focus on the form?
f   Are there any practice activities that focus on the meaning?
g   Do you like the material?
h   Do you think this material is suitable for the learners you are teaching? If not, in what ways could it be adapted?

8 Practising new language

A Warm-up

Read the following texts and answer the questions. Share your ideas with a partner.

1 Do you think that either of these learning experiences compares to the experience of learning a language? For example, what is the role of practice?
2 In your own experience in learning a second language, what kinds of practice were helpful?

> I remember having tennis lessons. We would spend ages just practising one shot – hitting backhands over and over again, or volleying at the net, or whatever. The lessons would always finish with a short match though – that was probably the bit I liked best.

> For me, being a chef is a dream job. As a kid I'd go into the kitchen and try to help my mum – chopping stuff up, that sort of thing. Then one day I just said 'I'll cook this', and I just got on with it. She gave advice now and then, but for the most part I learned by trying things out.

B Practice drills

Your trainer is going to give you a short foreign language lesson. After the lesson, discuss these questions in pairs:

1 Can you remember an instance of a choral drill (when all the class was drilled together)?
2 Can you remember examples of individual drills?
3 What was the purpose of the drills?
4 Was all the new language drilled? Why/why not?
5 How did you feel, being drilled?
6 Make two lists: the *pros* of drilling, and the *cons* of drilling. Compare your lists with other pairs.

C Written practice

1 Read exercises a–c and explain how they differ.

a

1 Complete the sentences with the words in the box.

texted	became	won	went	invited	bought

1 I .... to the supermarket yesterday and .... some bread, coffee and pizzas.
2 Paula .... me yesterday and .... me out.
3 Leona .... the talent competition and .... a big star.

b

1 Complete the sentences with the correct form of the words in the box.

text	become	win	go	invite	buy

1 I .... to the supermarket yesterday and .... some bread, coffee and pizzas.
2 Paula .... me yesterday and .... me out.
3 Leona .... the talent competition and .... a big star.

c

1 Complete the sentences.

1 I .... to the supermarket yesterday and .... some bread, coffee and pizzas.
2 Paula .... me yesterday and .... me out.
3 Leona .... the talent competition and .... a big star.

2 Explain how these practice exercises are different from drills. What advantages do they have?

3 Read exercise d. Is it more or less controlled than exercises a–c? Why? When might such an exercise be useful?

d

Write a sentence beginning with *if* for each of the following situations.
1 I was late for the interview. I didn't get the job.
   If ....
2 Wayne broke his foot. He didn't play in the final.
   If ....
3 The police officer dropped his gun. The prisoner escaped.
   If ....

4 Work in pairs. Write one controlled and one less controlled exercise to practise the distinction between *mustn't* (as in *You mustn't smoke*) and *don't have to* (as in *You don't have to wear a tie*).

D Interactive and communicative practice

1 Read activities a–e and complete the table that follows them by ticking the appropriate boxes.

a Dialogue to practise the past simple:

---

1 In pairs the learners practise the following dialogue:
  A: Hello Pat, Did you have a nice weekend?
  B: Yes. I went *skiing*.
  A: That sounds like fun. What was the weather like?
  B: It was *fantastic*. What about you? What did you do?
  A: I stayed at home. We *had a barbecue*.
  B: Was that fun?
  A: It was until I *burned myself!*
2 They change the elements in italics to make a new dialogue, and practise that.

---

b Circle drill to practise the present perfect:

The learners sit in a circle. The teacher shows the first picture (the Eiffel Tower) to a learner and asks 'Have you ever been to France?' The learner answers; the teacher gives the picture to the learner who turns to the next learner and asks the same question and then passes the picture on. The teacher then continues with the other pictures, so that all the pictures are travelling around the circle with the learners asking and answering questions.

c Spot the difference to practise *have got* and *there is*:
Learners work in pairs. They have very similar pictures, with only six differences. They take turns to ask each other questions in order to find the six differences between the two pictures.

d Find someone who … to practise *can*:
Learners stand up and mingle, asking questions so as to find people who can do the different activities. They then report back to the class.

> FIND SOMEONE WHO …
> can swim
> can speak more than three languages
> can juggle
> can play the piano
> can sing
> can drive a car

e Writing sentences to practise the future perfect:
In pairs the learners write as many true sentences as they can to complete this table.

By the end of next ….	we both will have	been to …
	one of us will have	done …
	neither of us will have	finished …
		etc.

	Dialogue	Circle drill	Spot the difference	Find someone who …	Writing sentences
There is built-in repetition: the activity gives learners opportunities to use the new language item on several occasions.					
The language is contextualised.					
Learners interact and/or take turns.					
Learners communicate: they must speak and listen to what is said.					
The language is personalised.					
The activity is fun and playful.					

B Classroom teaching

2 Explain the possible advantages of a practice activity that is:
   a repetitive
   b contextualised
   c interactive
   d communicative
   e personalised
   f fun

Think about the following questions. Then work in groups and compare your answers.
a Why do learners need to practise language if they already know the rules?
b How would you respond if learners made errors in the sort of activities you have seen in this unit?
c As well as the sort of practice activities you have seen in this unit, what other types of practice activity would you need for a balanced lesson?
d Is there a correct order for sequencing practice activities? What factors might influence a teacher's decision as to which practice activities to use, and when?

Less restricted exercises are dealt with in Unit 13.

9 Error correction

A Warm-up

1 Decide which teacher's views you agree with. Then work in groups and compare your ideas.

Olga:

> Errors need to be avoided at all costs. I don't want my learners to pick up bad habits.

Mariagrazia:

> Errors are a natural part of the learning process – and as teaching material they're really useful.

Paula:

> I feel bad correcting my students' errors – it's judgemental and de-motivating.

2 Think back to your own language learning experience. Did you like it when the teacher corrected your errors? Why? / why not? Compare experiences with a partner.

B Types of error

1 Find the errors in sentences 1–6 and match them with the classifications (a–f). Then compare your answers with a partner.

Errors	Classification
1 'She likes her job. She works for the same company for years.'	a problem with word stress
2 (In a restaurant) 'Bring me the menu!'	b problem with intonation
3 'My brother fell off his bike but he wasn't badly damaged.'	c problem with word order
4 'It's a lovely day, isn't it?'	d problem with choice of word(s) – vocabulary
5 'This sofa is very comFORTable.'	e problem with register
6 'Where is standing the teacher?'	f problem with the choice of verb form

2 Recall some of the errors that your learners have made in teaching practice. Do their errors fit one of the types above, or are they different?

C When to correct

Read the lesson transcripts. What should the teacher do about the learners' errors? Choose the best answer for each lesson. Then compare ideas with a partner.

a The teacher should not correct the error.
b The teacher should delay correction – and provide feedback at the end of the activity.
c The teacher should correct the error immediately.

Lesson 1

The students are working in different groups. The teacher is walking around the class, monitoring, and hears these utterances from speakers in the different groups.

S1: Technology is such important for all of us.
S2: In my country, everyone uses computers …
S3: Yeah, I am agree with Anja.
S4: I prefer to text friends than email them.

Lesson 2

T: And what's your job, Freddie?
S: I work in hotel. My job is to make the guests.

Lesson 3

T: We have a new student today. Vera, can you introduce yourself?
S: I am coming from Moscow. I am absolutely happy to join this class.

Lesson 4

The students have just listened to a recorded interview.
T: OK – what instrument does he play?
S: He is play saxophone.

D Correction strategies

1 Work in pairs. Compare the ways that different teachers responded to the same error. Explain their strategies.

S: We go to the beach yesterday.
  a T1: Yesterday – so, grammar?
  b T2: Yesterday, you ….
  c T3: Not quite, look: We go to the beach yesterday. [Holds up hand and indicates second finger from left from the learners' point of view.]
  d T4: Sorry, do you mean you go every day?
  e T5: You went to the beach – that's nice. Who did you go with?
  f T6: makes no comment; the activity continues until, at the end, the teacher says, 'I heard someone say, "We go to the beach yesterday." Can anyone correct that?'

2 Think about lessons you have observed. Did the teacher use any of the strategies in D1? If so, were they effective?

3 Complete the table.

Correction strategy	Advantages	Disadvantages
a Teacher prompts using terminology, e.g. *grammar, tense, pronunciation*, etc.	Easy to use. Indicates the type of error that the learner should be looking for.	Learners need to be familiar with the terminology used.
b Teacher repeats the utterance to the point of the error. e.g. *Yesterday you ...*		
c Finger correction (Teacher uses fingers to indicate the position of the error.)		
d Teacher asks a question, e.g. *Do you mean you go every day?*		
e Reformulation, e.g. *You went to the beach.*		
f Delayed correction		

E Demonstration

1 Read out the error on the card you are given and respond to what your trainer does or says. Pay attention to how the trainer corrects the error.

2 Look at the list of errors and complete the table.

Error	How was it corrected?
Can you borrow me some money?	
Do you can juggle?	
Bring me the menu!	
Where is going Felipe?	
Her father is a PROfessor.	
My brother fell off his bike but he wasn't badly damaged.	

F Classroom application

Work in groups of three. Your trainer will give you a set of cards. Each card has an error on it.

Trainee A: Play the role of the learner. Take a card and read out the error.
Trainee B: Play the role of the teacher. Correct A's error.
Trainee C: Play the role of an observer. Give feedback on the success of the correction strategy.

Take turns at playing each role.

REFLECTION

Work in pairs. Complete the mind map. You may add as many extra 'bubbles' as you wish. Then compare your mind map with another pair's.

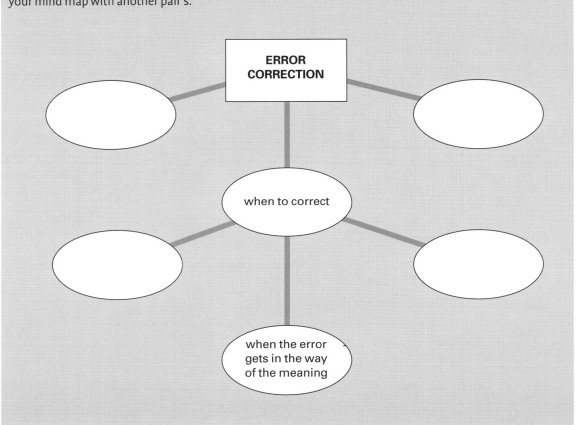

ERROR CORRECTION

when to correct

when the error gets in the way of the meaning

10 Developing listening skills

A Warm-up

1 Work in pairs. Write a list of all the things you listened to in the last 24 hours. For example:
- watching the news on TV last night
- listening to voicemail

2 Decide which of your 'listening experiences':
  a involved you speaking as well as listening, i.e. which were *interactive,* as opposed to those which were 'one-way', i.e. *non-interactive*
  b involved listening to a speaker who was physically present
  c involved listening for specific information
  d involved listening more for pleasure or entertainment
  e required you to listen closely and attentively
  f allowed a less attentive style of listening.

3 Rate these types of listening in terms of their likely difficulty for a second language learner:
- watching the news on TV
- listening to the news on the radio
- listening to a song on the radio
- talking about the news with a friend face to face
- talking about the news with a friend on the phone
- listening to a recording of the news in the classroom.

B Comprehension

1 Listen to your trainer reading two (unrelated) texts. Then answer the questions.
  1 Did you understand all the words in the texts?
  2 Did you understand the overall meaning of the texts?

2 Now listen again, and answer these questions.
  1 What was different about each text, the second time you heard it? Were the texts easier to understand?
  2 What factors make comprehension easier or more difficult?
  3 What are the implications of this activity on listening and reading in the classroom?
  4 What can the teacher do to make comprehension easier?

C Listening texts and tasks

1 Match each listening text type (1–8) with appropriate tasks (a–k). There are often several tasks which would be suitable for each text type.

Listening text types	Listening tasks
1 a news broadcast 2 the directions to a person's home 3 the description of a missing person 4 an embarrassing personal anecdote 5 a shopping dialogue (sales assistant and customer) 6 a pop song 7 recorded entertainment information (e.g. movies, theatre, etc.) 8 a weather forecast	a answering *wh*-questions (*where?, who?, what?, why?*, etc.) b putting a series of pictures in order c ticking off items on a list of names of people and places d drawing on a map e filling in a grid or table f choosing one of several pictures g taking notes h choosing one of several adjectives i writing the exact words j drawing a picture k filling in gaps in a transcript

2 Compare ideas with a partner. Explain your criteria for choosing tasks.

D A listening lesson

1 Read the coursebook extract and identify the purpose of the activities marked with an arrow (➞).

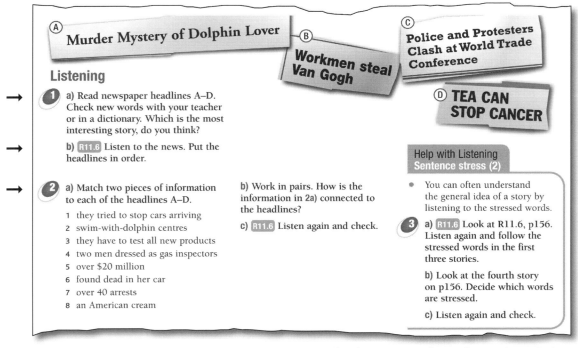

face2face (Pre-Intermediate) Redston and Cunningham

2 Put these stages of a listening task into a logical order.

a The teacher focuses on features of grammar or vocabulary that occur in the recording, e.g. by asking students to complete a gapped transcript.

b The teacher sets a task that requires listening for specific details. She plays the complete recording, checks the answers, and replays sections if necessary.

c Learners read the transcript of the recording and listen at the same time.

d The teacher generates interest in the topic by, for example, asking the class about their experience of, feelings on, or knowledge about, the topic.

e The teacher presents some key vocabulary in the listening text – for example, by giving, or eliciting, a definition or an example.

f The teacher sets a gist listening task – for example, *Who is talking to whom, about what, and why?* She then plays a short section of the recorded extract, and checks the answers.

3 Explain the principles underlying your order.

For example:
  • Learners will listen with more attention if their interest has been aroused (d).

E Classroom application

1 Put the stages in activity D2 in the correct column.

Pre-listening tasks	While-listening tasks	Post-listening tasks

2 Work in groups. Design a sequence of tasks for the following recorded text (in which people are talking about their jobs) that you could use with a group of pre-intermediate learners. Include at least one pre-listening task, one or more while-listening tasks, and one post-listening task.

NIGEL I became a pilot about 20 years ago. I had to do 72 weeks' basic training, but I didn't have to pay for it – the company did. I was lucky, I suppose, and now I have a job that I love. But these days most pilots have to pay a lot of money to do their training.

GARY You don't have to go to university, but you probably learn more facts than a university student – at least that's what people say! A London taxi driver has to know 25,000 streets and all the important places in the city.

MELISSA It's not easy to become a vet. You have to have a degree and the training takes 5 years. And you don't have much free time when you're a student vet – you have to work very hard.

face2face (Pre-Intermediate) Redston and Cunningham

B Classroom teaching

Read the questions and suggest some answers.

Questions about listening posted by teachers on a website discussion list.

Q1: How important is listening? My students just want to speak.

Q2: My students hate listening to recordings. Is there an acceptable alternative, such as reading the transcripts to them aloud?

Q3: When I do a listening activity in class, the students get frustrated if they can't understand every word. How can I discourage them from trying to do this?

Q4: My students say that they like listening to songs, but I'm not sure that this is a good idea. Should I let them, and, if so, is there an effective way of using songs?

Q5: Many coursebook listening texts sound a bit stilted and unnatural. Is there a good reason for this, and is there a viable alternative?

Q6: My students complain that they can understand recordings in the classroom, but that they have problems understanding real people when they talk to them. How can I help them with this?

11 Developing reading skills

A Warm-up

Read the statements and decide whether you agree or disagree. Compare ideas with a partner.

a Reading is like listening, except that the input is written, not spoken.
b Comprehension means understanding all the words in a text.
c Reading, in the classroom, means reading aloud.
d For teaching purposes, texts should be simplified.
e Reading is a good way of improving vocabulary.
f The aim of classroom reading is the appreciation of literary texts.
g If you can read well in your first language, you'll probably be able to read well in a second one.

B Reading purposes and strategies

1 Identify the reasons for reading and the ways of reading for these different text types.

Text type	Reason for reading		Way of reading		
	pleasure	information	close reading	skimming for gist	scanning for specific information
the instructions for installing a computer monitor		✓			
a text message (SMS) from a friend					
the evening's programmes in a TV guide					
a newspaper report of a sports event					
a short story					
a research paper published in a scholarly journal					

2 Discuss how the purpose of a text influences the way it is read.

C Reading in a second language

1 Read this text in Esperanto and answer the questions.

1 What kind of text is it?
2 What happened, and where? Where is this place exactly?
3 How many people died? How many survived?
4 What was happening at the time?

Fajro en teatro provokas la morton de 32 personoj en Egiptio

Incendio en teatro de la egipta urbo Beni-Suajfo, situanta 150 kilometrojn for de la ĉefurbo Kairo, falĉis la vivon de 32 personoj kaj vundis dekojn, laŭ informoj de la loka polico, jue ĉi tiu mardo. Proksimume 100 personoj estis en la teatro, ĝuante spektaklon, kiam fajro ekestis.

La fajrobrigadanoj sukcesis estingi la fajron, sed pluraj personoj pereis, plejparte surtretitaj de la panikiĝinta homamaso. "Ankaŭ estas mortigitoj pro asfiksio", diris la urbestro de Beni-Suajfo, Anaso Ĵafar. La urbo egipta estis la sidejo de festivalo pri amatora teatro, kio arigis plurajn aktorojn kaj trupojn el la tuta nordafrika lando.

(from the Esperanto website www.gxangalo.com)

2 Compare ideas with a partner.

1 How many questions could you answer? What clues were you using in order to answer them?
2 What does this tell you about reading in a second language?
3 What can the teacher do to help learners understand a text like the one above?

D Coursebook reading texts and tasks

1 Identify the purpose of tasks a–h in this coursebook extract. Decide whether they are *pre-reading*, *while-reading* or *post-reading* exercises.

■ Unit 7

SKILLS

Reading

1 Look at the photograph of Vanuatu.

a) What can you see?
b) Imagine you are there. What can you hear? What can you smell? What can you taste? How do you feel?
c) The words in the box are from Brian's article about Vanuatu. Use a dictionary to check the meaning.

paradise *(n)*	tiny *(adj)*	thoughts *(n)*
memory *(n)*	lucky *(adj)*	earthquake *(n)*

d) 📼 Do you think Brian was happy in Vanuatu? Read his article and check.
e) Answer the questions.

1 What can you say about Vanuatu?

- Where is it?
- What's the capital city?
- How many people live there?
- What's the weather like?

2 How did Brian get to work?
3 What do you think his job was?
4 What did he like eating in restaurants?
5 He remembers four bad things. What are they?
6 In England, which two things take Brian back to Paradise?

f) What colour does Brian use for:

1 the sea and the sky? 2 the sand? 3 the mountains? 4 the sun? 5 Britain?

g) Who or what ...

1 is sandy? 2 are kind and hardworking? 3 is slow? 4 is delicious? 5 is cold? 6 is sweet? 7 are fresh?

h) Imagine you're staying in Vanuatu. Write a postcard to a friend. Begin:
Dear ...
Here we are in Vanuatu. It's beautiful. The sea and the sky are very blue and ...

MY PARADISE

I was in Paradise when I lived in Vanuatu. Look at the map and you'll see a group of tiny islands in the Pacific Ocean. Look into my thoughts
5 and you'll see memories of those islands – of the wind in the palm trees, the blue sea and sky, the hot white sandy beaches and green mountains. I remember picnics on the beach and the fire-red sun going
10 down over the sea in the evening. I remember people, too, kind people who always smiled and worked hard. I remember visiting schools, going on foot up and down mountains or by boat to
15 other islands.

I was one of ten thousand lucky people who lived in Port Vila, the capital of Vanuatu. Life there was warm, friendly and slow. We played sports
20 slowly, sailed slowly to other islands, ate delicious seafood slowly in French restaurants and cooked meat very slowly on stones outside.

But there were problems, too. Once I
25 was very ill. There were hurricanes which blew down houses. There was a plane which crashed just after it took off. And once an earthquake carried my car across the road.

30 But now I'm back in cold, grey Britain I don't remember the bad things. I can taste the sweetness of the fruit. I can smell the freshness of the flowers. I can hear the wind in the trees. And when I
35 remember the colour and the sunlight, I'm in Paradise again.

Elementary Matters Bell and Gower

2 Work in groups. Imagine that you are going to use the following text with a group of intermediate learners.

   a Decide which features might help understanding and which might make it difficult to understand.

   b Design at least one *pre-reading*, one *while-reading*, and one *post-reading* task to use with this text.

   Then compare ideas with another group.

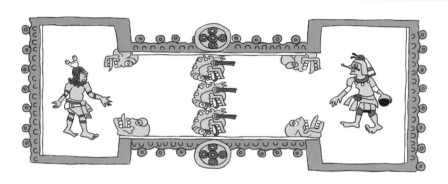

Pok-a-tok:
THE MEXICAN BALL GAME

From ancient times a ritual ball game was played by all the peoples of Mexico and Central America. The ruins of almost every ancient city include a walled court that was used for this sacred game. In Mexico alone well over 600 stone ball courts have been found.

The game (called *pok-a-tok* by the Aztecs) is no longer played and the rules were never written down. What we know about it is based on drawings and on descriptions by the first European visitors. Apparently, the players were divided into two teams. Each team fought for possession of the ball. On either side of the rectangular court were two long sloping walls. The object of the game was to drive the ball through rings that were positioned on these walls. The ball was solid rubber, probably a little larger than a modern basketball, and would have weighed several kilograms. The rings were almost identical in diameter to the balls, which must have made it extremely difficult to score. It seems that the first team to score won.

The players were not allowed to hit the ball with their hands or feet. They could use only their knees, hips and elbows. The ball could not touch the ground. Ballplayers used cotton pads and thick leather clothing to protect themselves from the ball. Evidently, players were often injured, despite these protective measures.

The game seems to have had a religious significance. It may have been a re-enactment of an ancient creation myth. Perhaps the ball symbolised the sun as it moved from the east to the west across the sky. If played correctly, the game would cause the sun to shine, the rain to come at the right time, and the crops to grow.

E A reading lesson

1 Put these stages of a reading lesson in a logical order. Then compare your answers with a partner.

a Check detailed understanding by asking multiple choice questions.

b Focus on vocabulary in the text by asking learners to find words that mean X, Y, Z.

c Use a picture to generate interest in the topic.

d Ask learners to read the text quickly in order to answer gist questions, such as: *What's it about? Who wrote it? Why?*

e Ask learners to talk about their personal response to the text and its topic.

f Teach essential vocabulary that learners may be unfamiliar with.

g Focus on a grammar structure in the text by, for example, asking learners to underline each instance of it.

h Use the title of the text to encourage learners to predict the content of the text.

2 Choose a reading text in a coursebook that you are using.

a Identify any *pre-*, *while-*, and *post-reading* tasks.

b Using ideas from activity E1, could you add anything to the sequence of tasks?

REFLECTION

Work in groups. Discuss these questions.

a What is the advantage of choosing reading texts that are accompanied by illustrations, diagrams, or maps?

b What are the advantages of using real (i.e. authentic) texts rather than texts that have been specially written or adapted for classroom purposes?

c Why is setting a task in advance of reading a good idea?

d What does 'matching the task to the text' mean? Why is it a good idea?

e Why is it sometimes a good idea to let learners compare their answers to reading comprehension questions?

f Should learners be allowed to consult dictionaries while reading? What is the alternative?

g Should learners answer comprehension questions from memory, or should they be allowed to consult the text? Why? / Why not?

12 Presenting language through texts

A Warm-up

1 Match the two halves of these sentences:

Grammar presentation: review	
1 When presenting a new grammar item, you can convey the meaning of the new item	a by eliciting true sentences that incorporate the new item.
2 And you can highlight the form of the item	b by asking concept checking questions.
3 Then you can check understanding of the new item	c by writing it on the board or having students repeat it.
4 Finally, you can provide initial practice of the item	d through a real or imaginary situation.

2 Read the example, and then suggest two other ways of presenting the same structure.

> Target structure: *She's been doing X for Y days/weeks/months, etc. now.*
>
> **Teacher:** [points to picture] This is Lisa. She used to be a receptionist in a hotel. But she changed her job six months ago. She did a course in acupuncture. Now she works as an acupuncturist. She's been doing this for six months now.

B Context

1 Meaning becomes clearer in context. But some contexts are better than others. Choose the best context (a–d) to present *have to* (obligation).

1 Which context best shows the meaning?
2 Which context best shows the form? Why?

a
> Amy: Hi, Bella. Would you like to come over tomorrow evening?
> We're having a few friends round to play Scrabble.
> Bella: Gee thanks, but I can't. I have to babysit for my sister. Thanks all the same.
> Amy: Never mind. Some other time, maybe.

b
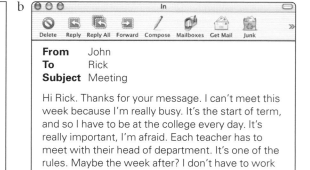

From   John
To   Rick
Subject Meeting

Hi Rick. Thanks for your message. I can't meet this week because I'm really busy. It's the start of term, and so I have to be at the college every day. It's really important, I'm afraid. Each teacher has to meet with their head of department. It's one of the rules. Maybe the week after? I don't have to work on Monday: I'm free all day.

c

> I often have to go to London, and when I do I usually stay with friends. Next month I have to go again. This time I'm going to stay in a hotel, because my company is paying. It's also more convenient because it's in the centre of London, whereas my friends live miles out.

d

> Ann: Hi, Bill. What do you have to do tomorrow?
> Bill: I have to go to my math class. And then I have to prepare for an exam. What do you have to do?
> Ann: I have to practise the violin. Then I have to go to school. After school I have to do my homework.
> Bill: You've got a busy day!

2 Write down two or three principles for choosing, or designing, contexts for language presentation.

C Text-based presentations

1 Read the first part of the extract from a coursebook (about Tanya) and answer the questions.

 1 What structure is this text presenting?
 2 Does the text provide a useful context for it?

1 Read about how Tanya describes her life and her dream.

Tanya, aged 7
I live in a block of flats with my Mum and little brother. My Mum works in a hospital, and so my Gran often looks after us and helps my Mum. We have a budgie and a goldfish. I go to St Paul's School and I wear a blue and grey uniform.

If... If I were a princess, I'd live in a palace. If I lived in a palace, I'd have servants to look after me. My Mum would be Queen, and she wouldn't work. I wouldn't go to school, I'd have a governess. I'd ride a white horse and I'd wear a long dress and a gold crown.

Headway (Pre-Intermediate) Soars and Soars

● Grammar questions

– Which tense is used to describe Tanya's real life?
– *If I lived in a palace, ...*
  Does she live in a palace?
  What tense is **lived**?
– *... I'd have servants to look after me.*
  Is this a dream or reality?
– Complete the following rule.
  The Second Conditional is formed with **if** + the
  _____ tense, the auxiliary verb _____ + the
  _____ without **to**.

2 Practise the sentences that express Tanya's dream.

3 Read about how Graham describes his life, and complete the sentences about his dream.

Graham, aged 9
I live in a cottage in a village near Glasgow. My Dad is unemployed and my Mum works in a pub in the city. I go to the village school. I walk to school with my friend. We often play football together. I have a cat and some chickens.

If... If I _____ a prince, I _____ in a castle. I _____ in a cottage. My Dad _____ King, and my Mum _____ in a pub. A chauffeur _____ me to school. I _____ polo on a white horse. I _____ peacocks in my garden. I _____ chickens.

2 Read the follow-up to the text in activity C1 (labelled 'Grammar questions') and identify the purpose of each stage.

Headway (Pre-Intermediate) Soars and Soars

D Classroom application

1 Work in pairs or groups. Read one of the following authentic texts and decide:

a what language area(s) you could present using your text, at the level that is indicated

b how you would stage your presentation, including preliminary work on helping the learners understand the text.

Text a: level: Elementary/Pre-intermediate

Backpacker  **Q&A**

NAME JOSH KIPPIN
AGE 21 **FROM** OTTAWA, CANADA

How long have you been here for?
I came to London about a month ago with my friend after an inter-railing trip around Europe.

Wow! Inter-railing sounds great. Where did you go?
We went pretty much everywhere. I think Barcelona was probably my favourite place.

Are you planning on working while you're here?
Yeah, we both have working visas. My friend has a job in a bar but I'm still looking. I think I should get one soon. We drink a lot – I think that is where my money seems to be disappearing to.

That could be it. So you're enjoying what London has to offer, then?
Yeah, we love it. Everyone is really friendly and there's so much to do. It's been great meeting other backpackers in and around the hostel.

How long do you plan to stick around?
I think we will probably stay as long as we can. After this we're heading back home.

No more travelling expeditions, then?
Maybe in the future. I'd love to go to Japan and my girlfriend is heading to New Zealand next year, so I'm hoping to get out there at some point.

Sounds great. So what's been your best memory of London so far?
Probably when we first arrived. I remember feeling really excited and couldn't wait to be part of London life; it's been great. I think I'll definitely be back in the future.

– JENNIFER ARNOTT

(from article by Jennifer Arnott, TNT Magazine)

Text b: level: Mid-intermediate

Transports of delight

A Suffolk woman travelled from John o'Groats to Land's End – using 73 different types of transport.

Roz Gordon, 35, headed south on a dog sled, pogo stick, unicycle, and even a camel on her six-week 1,162-mile trip.

She also travelled by ambulance, canoe, catamaran, Rolls-Royce, go-kart, golf buggy, kayak, lawn mower, luggage trolley, pedalo, quad bike, rickshaw, skateboard, stilts, stretcher, tricycle, wheelbarrow and many more.

The landscape photographer used each method for at least 100 metres and a maximum of 50 miles.

She completed her journey in 183 stages.

Roz told the Mirror: 'When you arrive in a town on a Space hopper or pogo stick you quickly lose your inhibitions.'

She finished the trek with a piggyback from her brother Phil, 39.

Roz, of Wenhaston, Suffolk, raised £3,270 for Ataxia UK. Her mum Sandra, 67, suffers from the condition.

(from web article www.ananova.com)

Text c: level: Upper Intermediate

LEO
July 24th–
August 23rd

Mistakes made are not beyond repair no matter what other people are telling you. You might feel half tempted to walk away from a stressful situation but if you do, nothing will be resolved and you will only have the same issue to return to later. A responsible attitude and perseverance will be the way to work out a solution. As you take charge others will realise you aren't called the Lion of the zodiac for nothing! Call my Leo advice line 0905 062 3000 to hear why you can be a major motivator for others and how you will get good news by the weekend.

CAPRICORN
December 22nd–
January 20th

Although your boss or a superior isn't in a good mood, don't keep anything from them. You want to use your initiative to sort out a tricky matter without consulting anyone. This could lead to a dressing down when a manager disagrees. Granted, others may grumble and groan if you take problems to them. You might even feel a complete idiot at having to rely on their involvement but it's one of those days when you just can't win no matter what you do! Call my Capricorn advice line 0905 062 3000 to hear why you need to remember your most important commitment is to yourself.

PISCES
February 20th–
March 20th

If you receive an unexpected financial gift or some other kind of money surprise, don't be too quick to spend it! It could turn out there are strings attached or you were not the proper recipient for this after all. You don't want to have to pay for other people's mistakes but if you act too quickly or take anything for granted, it is entirely possible that is what's going to happen, today. Call my Piscean advice line 0905 062 3000 to hear why an unusual achievement or unexpected success will boost your personal prestige and reputation.

(from web horoscope www.russellgrant.com)

2　Demonstrate your presentation to the rest of the class.

REFLECTION

Work in groups. Discuss these questions:

a　What are the advantages of using a text-based presentation, compared to other approaches?
b　What are some of the possible problems?
c　What advantages and disadvantages would there be in using authentic texts (as opposed to specially written texts) for presentation purposes?

13 Developing speaking skills

A Warm-up

1 Walk around the room and talk to as many different people as possible. Ask questions to find three people that you have at least three things in common with. You can only count things that you do not already know. For example, *We are both female* is not valid for this activity.

2 Answer the questions.

1 What assumptions does this activity make about language level and learners?
2 What skills does this activity practise?
3 What is the teacher's role here?
4 Would this activity be appropriate for the learners that you are teaching?
5 If you used this activity, how would you round it off?

> This unit focuses on fluency based speaking activities. More controlled, or restricted, activities are dealt with in Unit 8.

B Different speaking activities

Communicative language teaching is based on the premise that people use language in order to communicate. As we communicate by speaking, listening, reading and writing, then it follows that it is useful to give direct practice in these skills – rather than using these skills only as a means of practising particular language points.

1 Discuss the questions for the speaking activities 1–5 on the following pages. Then complete the table on page 58.

a Is it practical? Consider how easy the activity is to set up and manage. For example, does it need any materials? Do the learners need time to prepare?
b Is it purposeful? Do the learners have a purpose for doing the activity? Is there an outcome?
c Is it productive? How much speaking will it generate?
d Is it predictable? How easy is it to predict the language that the learners will need in order to do the activity? For example, what vocabulary and grammar are they likely to need?
e Is it adaptable? How versatile is the activity type? For example, could you adapt it for a higher or lower level?

Activity 1

Discussion

Work in groups. Discuss the following quotations. Do you agree or disagree with them? Give reasons.

A teacher should have maximal authority and minimal power. (Thomas Szasz)
We teachers can only help the work going on, as servants wait upon a master. (Maria Montessori)
Technology is just a tool. In terms of getting the kids working together and motivating them, the teacher is the most important. (Bill Gates)

Activity 2

Roleplay

A parent is concerned because their 8-year-old child is unhappy at school. The parent will meet the teacher and the headteacher of the school. You will take one of the following roles.

Student A: Parent
You are worried that your child is unhappy at school. You think she is being bullied by older children. You have been very busy at work lately and only noticed the problem recently although your daughter says that it has existed for some time.

Student B: Teacher
You have only been working at the school a few months. You know that a parent is coming to see you and the headteacher about their daughter. You are pleased they are coming, because the girl has been disruptive in lessons.

Student C: Headteacher
You are going to have a meeting with the parent of one of the children and her teacher. You will run the meeting. You do not know a lot about this child, but you know that her former teacher felt that she was doing well. The girl's current teacher has only recently joined your team.

1 **Work with another student who has the same role as you. Plan what you are going to say.**
2 **In groups of three (A, B and C), act out the roleplay.**

Activity 3

Survey and presentation

1 **In groups of four, prepare a survey on the topic:** *Are you a good language learner?*
   Prepare six questions that you will ask the other students in the class.
   For example: *Do you do the homework that the teacher gives us?*
   a Always   b Sometimes   c Never.
2 **Form new groups, so that each student in the new group comes from one of the original groups. Ask the other students your questions, and make a note of their answers.**
3 **Return to your original group. Share the results of your survey. Prepare a presentation of your findings. Use expressions like** *Five out of ten students always do their homework.* **Draw some conclusions from your survey. For example,** *It would be good if we could listen to more songs in English. This would improve our listening skills…*
4 **Take turns to present your findings and conclusions to the class.**

Activity 4

Guessing game

1 **Write six sentences about your typical daily routine. Some sentences should be true and some should be false.**
2 **Work in groups of three. Take turns to read out one sentence each. Can you guess which of your classmates' sentences are true or false? If you are not sure, you can ask them questions.**

Activity 5

Information gap

1 **This is your diary for next week. Fill in five of the spaces with arrangements you have made. For example:** *meeting with boss*; *dental appointment.*

	morning	afternoon
MONDAY		
TUESDAY		
WEDNESDAY		
THURSDAY		
FRIDAY		

2 **You need to arrange a meeting with two colleagues. Work in groups of three. Use your diaries to find a time when you can all meet.**

	a Is it practical?	b Is it purposeful?	c Is it productive?	d Is it predictable?	e Is it adaptable?
1 Discussion					
2 Roleplay					
3 Survey and presentation					
4 Guessing game					
5 Information gap					

2 Work in pairs. Choose one of the exercises from activity B1. Decide how you would set it up in class. Write down the instructions you would use.

C Challenges

1 Look at these comments about speaking by learners. What could their teachers do to help?

Cinzia (intermediate learner from Italy):

I quite like speaking lessons now. But I remember when I was just starting to learn English, I hated it when the teacher asked me to speak. I was scared I'd make too many mistakes.

Hyun-Joo (upper-intermediate learner from Korea):

I'm studying in Brighton – but I'm from Korea. My teacher often asks me to talk about what I think about politics, or crime or something. I don't really like talking about things like that in lessons. I don't think these are good subjects for an English lesson.

Danijela (advanced learner from Serbia):

I don't like roleplays much – I hate saying things that I don't really believe – I prefer to talk about real things.

Alejandra (intermediate learner from Chile):

I remember a teacher asked me in front of the whole class if it was a good idea to increase taxes to pay for more doctors. I don't know – I didn't know what to say – I don't know in Spanish!

Ali (elementary learner from Libya):

Outside the classroom, I find it difficult to speak sometimes because I know the English but I never know when the other people want me to say something. I always miss my turn!

Anja (advanced learner from Switzerland):

I don't really think I learn much from discussion in class – I can do that with my friends anyway and the teacher never corrects us when we make mistakes.

Vera (intermediate learner from Russia):

I don't like speaking lessons much because the other students are much better than me and I don't get a chance to say very much.

2   What can you learn from the learners in activity 1? Complete the table. Then compare ideas with a partner.

	What we can learn from the learner
Cinzia	
Hyun-Joo	
Danijela	
Alejandra	
Ali	
Anja	
Vera	

D Questions and answers

1 Match these postings on a web-based teachers' discussion board with the responses.

QUESTIONS

1 If you could give one tip to a new teacher doing speaking lessons – what would it be?

2 What should I do at the end of pairwork and groupwork?

3 Should I feel guilty if there's no specific language point practised in a speaking exercise?

4 I taught a lesson last week and it started and finished with some speaking. But the two speaking tasks were nearly the same. Is that OK?

5 I can't always hear what the learners are saying. Does anyone else have this problem? What can you do?

6 Should I correct learners when I hear a mistake?

RESPONSES

a If you use groups of three or four, learners have to speak a bit louder than when they are working in pairs.

b No. You can't always restrict people to using particular forms. Correction is a way of focusing on a variety of language points, anyway.

c Shut up! It took me ages to learn that. I'd ask a question and before anyone else spoke I'd answer my own question. I was terrified of silence. Also if learners are talking, doing what you want them to do – don't interrupt them and stop them doing it.

d Typically, two things. One, get some of the learners to report back on what they discussed. Two, give them some feedback on how they said it – good stuff, mistakes, you know…

e Well, I often give some feedback afterwards and may correct errors then, but I try to interrupt as little as possible – unless the error is so bad that it stops communication.

f I often have the same conversations! I think it can be a good thing – the learners should see an improvement, which is good. Sometimes I just switch the groups round a bit so that they are not talking to the same people.

2 Are there any other questions you would like to ask about speaking skills lessons?

> Dealing with errors is dealt with in Unit 9.

REFLECTION

Work with a partner from another teaching practice group. Look at the books that you are using with your respective groups and choose one speaking activity from each. Answer the following questions.

a Do you like the material? Would you be happy to use it with the appropriate group?

b Choose one of the activities. How could you make it maximally productive? For example, how could you ensure that as many learners as possible are speaking as much of the time as possible?

c Write the stages you would go through in order to exploit it.

14 Developing writing skills

A Warm-up

1 All of the following comments were made by practising teachers. Which ones do you agree with? Discuss your ideas in groups.

a Tracy:

> Writing in class is a waste of time. The learners may as well do it at home.

b Korali:

> I mainly use writing to practise grammar and vocabulary: learners are more accurate when they write than when they speak.

c David:

> I don't think you should correct every mistake when learners write something. I only pick out what I think are the main points and I always write comments saying what I liked about what was said, or what I thought was surprising and so on.

d Paula:

> Learners sometimes see writing as a chore. The most important thing is to make it fun and to encourage learners to express themselves.

e Hassan:

> Writing should be done individually, or else weaker writers will simply rely on the stronger ones.

B Writing activities

1 Complete the table on p 62 for activity types a–e below.

a Multiple-choice gap fill
The learners choose the best answer to complete sentences. For example:

> We had a nice holiday .... the weather was bad.
> a despite   b in spite of   c because   d although

b Reproducing a model
Learners study a model text and then write their own text based on it. For example, they read a letter of complaint and answer questions about the layout of the letter and the content of each paragraph. Afterwards they write their own letter of complaint.

c Interactive writing
Learners interact in writing. For example, they write, and respond to, text messages to each other.

d Composition
Learners write a composition. For example, they discuss the achievements of a famous person.

e Dialogue writing + items
Learners write a dialogue that includes pre-selected items. For example, they must include six words that are given by the teacher.

Analysis of activity types					
Activity type	Purpose: is there a communicative purpose to the task?	Integration: do the learners produce whole texts?	Authenticity: is the task a real-life one?	Readership: does the writer have a specific reader (or readers) in mind?	What level could it be used for?
a Gap fill					
b Reproducing a model					
c Interactive writing					
d Composition					
e Dialogue writing + items					

2 Work in pairs. Discuss ways to redesign the following writing task, in order to:

   a make it more communicative
   b make it more integrated (i.e. so that the learners are producing whole texts, not simply a list of sentences)
   c make it more authentic
   d provide a readership

   > **Write ten sentences describing your favourite pop group.**

C Stages in writing

1 Imagine writing an article for a teachers' journal. Put the stages below in the order in which you would do them. Are there any things here that you wouldn't do?

   a Read and make changes and corrections.
   b Write a rough draft.
   c Organise your ideas.
   d Consult books and talk to colleagues to get ideas.
   e Write a final copy.

2 We can see from activity C1 that writing involves a number of different processes. Discuss what implications this has for teaching.

3 Read this sequence of activities from a coursebook and answer the questions.
   1 What is the purpose of each stage?
   2 To what extent does the sequence reflect the processes of writing, as outlined in activity C1?

A formal e-mail

WRITING **5**

a Read the e-mail to a language school. Tick (✓) the questions that Adriano wants the school to answer.

☐ How much do the courses cost?
☐ When do the courses start and finish?
☐ How many students are there are in a class?
☐ Are there Business English classes?
☐ Where can I stay?
☐ Where are the teachers from?

b Look at the highlighted expressions. How would they be different in an informal e-mail (or letter)?

Formal e-mail	Informal e-mail
Dear Sir / Madam	_____
I am writing	_____
I would like	_____
I look forward to hearing from you	_____
Yours faithfully	_____

From: Adriano Ruocco [adrianor@tiscali.net]

To: The Grange Language School [enquiries@grangeedinburgh]
Subject: Information about courses

Dear Sir / Madam ,

I am writing to ask for information about your language courses. I am especially interested in an intensive course of two or three weeks. I am 31 and I work in the library at Milan University. I can read English quite well but I need to improve my listening and speaking. The book I am currently studying is 'pre-intermediate' (Common European Framework level A2).

I have looked at your website, but there is no information about intensive courses next summer. Could you please send me information about dates and prices? I would also like some information about accommodation. If possible I would like to stay with a family. My wife is going to visit me for a weekend when I am at the school. Could she stay with me in the same family?

I look forward to hearing from you.

Yours faithfully

Adriano Ruocco

---

c Read the advertisements and choose a course. Think of two or three questions you would like to ask.

Thai Cookery courses in Chiang Mai

Learn to cook Thai food in northern Thailand. One week courses, from April to October. Your accommodation in Chiang Mai is included. Beginners welcome. E-mail us for more information at thaicook@blueelephant.com

Tennis courses in France

One- or two-week courses in different parts of the country. Professional tennis coaches. All levels, beginners to advanced. Small groups or private lessons. For more information e-mail us at info@tennisinfrance.com

---

WRITE a formal e-mail asking for information. Write two paragraphs.
Paragraph 1 Explain why you are writing and give some personal information.
Paragraph 2 Ask your questions, and ask them to send you information.

CHECK your e-mail for mistakes (grammar , punctuation , and spelling).

New English File Oxenden, Latham-Koenig and Seligson

4 Suggest how you would adapt or supplement the material in activity C3.

D Marking written work

Work in pairs. Discuss the ways the errors in this learner writing have been indicated and answer the questions.

1 Which of the three ways do you think is the most effective?
2 The writer of this text is an intermediate learner. Do you think the approach to correction would be the same for all levels?
3 What do the symbols mean? Complete the key.

As you know, this product <u>is</u> on sale for four years and we want‿increase sale. We have some ideas for advertis<u>e</u> the product. Healthy products are fashi<u>n</u>able now and we should <u>to</u> focus on this.

         made
Our product is ~~make~~ from herbs and we can ~~to~~ tell people this. One of the ideal⌐is to changed the

                pronounce   believe   to   wrapper
name because now it is difficult to ~~pronunciate~~. Also we ~~belief~~ that we need⌐update the ~~wraps~~.

        T   G   +   SP   ww
Also, we are deciding the price should cheaper than competitors becuase we can do more market share
                        un
this way. In addition we should to be an official sponsor at the next Olympic Games. But
        ww
television publicity is also very important.

Key to symbols   ww = wrong word   wo =   T =   un =
                     sp = spelling   G =   P =   + =

E Classroom application

Work in small groups. Your trainer will assign your group one of the following writing tasks. Plan the stages of a lesson that lead up to the activity.

- Write a review of a film for a website for film buffs.
- Write an email to an online book distributor complaining about their failure to deliver a book.
- Write an account of an embarrassing incident for a teenage magazine.
- Write a reference for a colleague who has applied for a job or scholarship.

REFLECTION

1 Complete the following sentence in as many different ways as you can. Use one of the words in the box below in each sentence.

collaborative communicate practice process readership

To teach writing ...

2 Did you like this writing task? Would your learners like it? Adapt the activity so that it would be appropriate for a class that you are teaching.

15 Integrating skills

A Warm-up

1 Work in pairs. One is the reader and one is the writer. Reader: run to the wall and read the text. Run back to your partner and dictate as much of the text as you can remember. Continue until your partner has completed writing the text. Work as quickly as you can. When you have finished, compare your text with the original.

2 Work in pairs. Answer the questions about activity A1.

  1 What skills (speaking, listening, reading and writing) did you each practise?
  2 Did you enjoy the activity? What was the atmosphere like in the room as you were doing it?
  3 Would you be able to use this type of activity with a class you are teaching?

B Combining skills

1 Work in groups. Tick the skills that you think would be involved in each of the following activities.

Activity	listening	speaking	reading	writing
a Learners do a 15-minute roleplay in pairs. Half the class are journalists, who interview the other half of the class, who are famous actors.				
b Learners work briefly in small groups to discuss ideas to put into a piece of writing on animal rights. They then write a magazine-style article on the subject.				
c Learners read a text about language teaching methodologies and answer questions. They discuss their answers in small groups before reporting back to the teacher.				
d Learners read a short newspaper description of a radio programme. They then listen to the radio programme and answer questions.				
e Learners work in pairs to write a review of a restaurant they like.				
f Learners make notes as they listen to a short, recorded lecture.				

2 Choose one of the four skills and see where it occurs in the table in Activity B1.

1 Is it equally central to the activity in each case?

2 What implications might this have for teaching?

Choose some tasks in the coursebook you are using in teaching practice that include a combination of two skills. Consider the balance of the skills in the tasks. Are the skills equally prominent in all cases?

C Classroom application

Think of ways you could use this text in a lesson so that all four language skills are practised.

Aliens 'will chat to us in 20 years'

Aliens will be talking to us within the next 20 years, according to scientists. Dr Seth Shostak of the Search for Extra Terrestrial Intelligence group said: 'We'll know we are not alone between the years 2020 and 2025. This will be one of the biggest, if not the biggest, story of all time.' His group is building 350 telescopes to listen for ETs reports The Sun. Dr Shostak believes aliens could already be listening to Earth. And he reckons alien life may have landed in clumps of bacteria cells.

(from news website www.ananova.com)

D Integrating content and language

One way in which skills are very naturally integrated is in *content-based learning* (also called *content and language integrated learning* or *CLIL*). This is when the teacher teaches a subject – such as biology, economics, or geography (as in the lesson description below) – *through* English.

1 Read the lesson description and identify the skills practised. At what stage is there a focus on grammar?

a The teacher asks *Why is Brazil hotter than Greece? Why is Denmark colder than Greece?* The learners discuss the answers in pairs.

b The learners then read the following text:

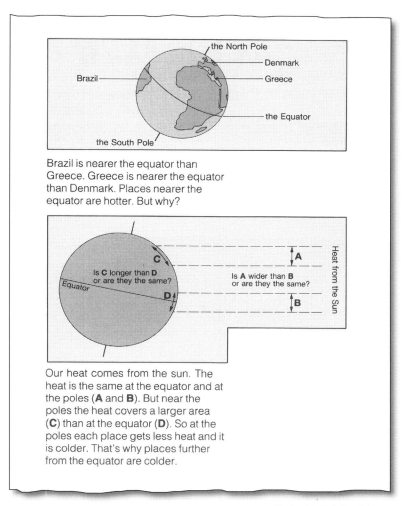

Brazil is nearer the equator than Greece. Greece is nearer the equator than Denmark. Places nearer the equator are hotter. But why?

Our heat comes from the sun. The heat is the same at the equator and at the poles (**A** and **B**). But near the poles the heat covers a larger area (**C**) than at the equator (**D**). So at the poles each place gets less heat and it is colder. That's why places further from the equator are colder.

Project English Hutchinson

c The teacher checks their understanding of the text by asking questions, and then asks the learners to use the pictures to explain to each other why some places are hotter than others.
d Learners match opposites in a list of comparative adjectives, such as *hotter – colder.*
e They then form comparatives from adjectives, like *wide – wider, big – bigger, wet – wetter, thin – thinner,* etc.
f They then read the text again, and underline the comparative forms.
g They then listen to the following recorded text, and do this task.

Look at these temperature graphs for four cities
Listen and match the temperature graphs with
the cities:

Which graph is for which city?

Moscow is hotter than London in July.
Only one city is colder than London in January.
Lisbon is always hotter than Moscow.
Madrid is hotter than Lisbon in April, but is
colder in February.

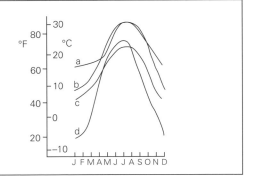

h Learners then collaborate on the following task.

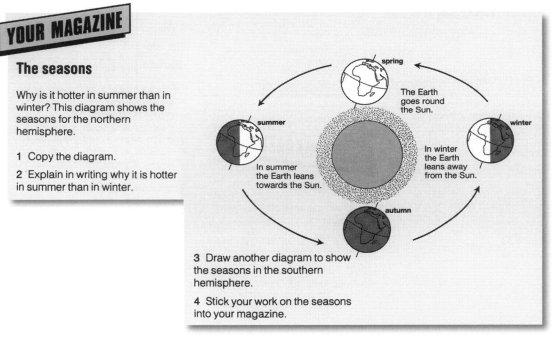

YOUR MAGAZINE

The seasons

Why is it hotter in summer than in
winter? This diagram shows the
seasons for the northern
hemisphere.

1 Copy the diagram.

2 Explain in writing why it is hotter
in summer than in winter.

The Earth
goes round
the Sun.

In winter
the Earth
leans away
from the Sun.

In summer
the Earth leans
towards the Sun.

3 Draw another diagram to show
the seasons in the southern
hemisphere.

4 Stick your work on the seasons
into your magazine.

Project English Hutchinson

2 Work in pairs. Answer the questions.

1 In what ways is the above sequence similar to / different from standard coursebook material?

2 What advantages can you see in content-based learning? Are there any disadvantages?

3 The above material was written for younger learners. Would the same approach work with a class of adults? What adaptations might you need to make?

REFLECTION

Work in pairs or groups of three. Read the rules and play the game.

Rules

- Each player needs a counter and should place it on the start line.
- Players flip a coin.
- If the coin lands on 'heads' they move one square, and if it lands on 'tails' they move two squares.
- When a player lands on a question square s/he should answer the question.
- If s/he does not answer to the satisfaction of the other player(s), s/he must go back to the square s/he moved from.

Skills quiz

START

1 What do you understand by 'receptive' skills?

2 What do you understand by 'productive' skills?

3 What is an 'authentic' text?

4 Why is it not necessary for learners to understand every word of a text?

5 How could you make a recorded listening text easier?

6 What do you understand by 'a process approach to writing'?

7 What other skill would you usually expect to find in a speaking lesson?

8 Explain how you could incorporate at least one other skill into a writing lesson.

9 Why might a teacher avoid asking low level classes to take notes while they listen?

10 Learners read a text about a holiday where everything went wrong. They answer questions based on the text. How could you also develop productive skills in this lesson?

11 Give some criteria that you might use in selecting an authentic text.

Congratulations

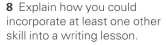
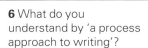

16 Lesson planning: design and staging

A Warm-up

1 Choose one of the following sentences and complete it.

    a A good lesson is like a film because …

    b A good lesson is like a football match because …

    c A good lesson is like a meal because …

    d A good lesson is like a symphony because …

2 Find somebody who chose the same sentence starter as you. Did you complete it in a similar way?

3 Consider teaching a sixty-minute lesson on the past simple with an elementary class. How could you apply your metaphor to the design of the lesson?

B Sequencing stages

Good lessons usually follow a logical sequence.

1 Work in pairs. Put these stages of a lesson into a logical order. How long would you expect to spend on each stage in a 45-minute lesson?

Level: Intermediate

Task: Writing a story to practise past simple and past continuous

Stage	Time	Procedure
		a The teacher divides the class into three groups. Each group makes up a story.
		b The teacher asks questions to check understanding.
1	0–5 mins	c The teacher asks learners about their favourite stories when they were young. Learners volunteer stories.
		d The teacher clarifies the form with examples (*she went / she was going*) on the board and then gives out a series of rules of use of the verb forms. Learners decide which rules go with which verb form and pick out examples from the text.
		e Learners complete sentences, deciding whether the past simple or continuous is more appropriate.
		f The teacher gives out a short story and asks learners to underline examples of the past simple in blue and examples of the past continuous in red.
		g The teacher forms new groups, comprising one person from each of the other groups. The learners tell each other their stories.

2 Compare your solution with another pair's. Explain why your order is logical.

C Planning decisions

Good lessons tend to have a variety of activities and pace. Part of achieving this depends on having different interaction patterns.

1 Complete the table with the interaction patterns in the box.

Ss–text   Ss–Ss   Ss–T   Ss–Ss

Activity	Procedure	Interaction
Speaking	Learners talk about their hobbies and interests in groups.	
Task checking/ Report back	Teacher asks the learners what they talked about.	
Reading for gist	Learners read a text quickly to understand the gist and answer questions.	
Checking answers	Learners compare answers to reading.	

2 Adapt or extend the following grammar exercise to encourage a variety of interaction patterns.

1   Make ten sentences from the box. Example:

My father is often bad-tempered.

I am _____ is _____ are	always usually often sometimes not often occasionally never	happy late tired friendly bad-tempered depressed worried in love in trouble *etc*

How English Works Swan and Walter

D Putting it on paper

Planning decisions are made about every lesson. However, some teachers like to plan more formally than others and some teaching situations may demand a more formal approach to planning. Written lesson plans can usually be divided into two parts. One part is the 'procedure' – it includes the activities, their rationale, and their interaction patterns (see sections B and C). The other part could be termed the 'pre-plan' and gives background to the lesson.

1 Match the terms 1–5 with the examples a–e.

Pre-plan	
1 Aims	a The learners already know *will* and may overuse this. If necessary I will use a short discrimination exercise contrasting *will* and *going to*.
2 Level	b 60 minutes
3 Length of lesson	c By the end of the lesson the learners will have practised expressing future plans using *going to* + infinitive.
4 Class profile	d Pre-intermediate
5 Anticipated problems/solutions	e There are ten students in the class. They are all Chinese (Mandarin) speakers and are aged 18–23.

2 Put the anticipated problems into the correct category.

   a The pairwork exercise requires an even number of learners. It's possible that one (or more) may not attend, leaving an odd number.
   b Fan Kong is much stronger than the other learners and tends to answer every question I ask.
   c Three or four learners tend to talk in Chinese if they're asked to do group/pair work.
   d Li Baoning is very shy and won't say anything unless asked directly.
   e Some learners have a problem with word stress and they are difficult to understand.

Linguistic	Organisational	Individual
The learners already know 'will' and may overuse this.		

3 Suggest solutions for the anticipated difficulties in activity D2.

   For example, *If necessary I will use a short discrimination exercise contrasting 'will' and 'going to'.*

E Procedures

Work in groups. Your trainer will give you the pieces of a lesson plan for the following lesson:

Aim: to present and practise '2nd' conditional to talk about hypothetical situations in present/future time (e.g. *If I had the time I would study Russian.*)

Class: Intermediate / adults.

Use the timings to establish the sequence of stages. Then match the activities and their rationales with each stage.

REFLECTION

Work in groups. Choose two or three of the following statements and discuss them. Who are you most like at the moment? Do you think you will change after the course?

Karina:

I never plan – I follow the coursebook. After all, it was written and trialled by experts.

Kaylea:

I plan … and plan and plan. I think I spend at least as much time planning as I do teaching. I do it because my students deserve a professional approach.

Tom:

I used to spend ages planning when I started teaching – but I've got more experienced so I feel I don't need to.

Maria:

I plan the first five minutes or so – just a speaking activity, something to get them going – and then I pick out some grammar, some vocabulary from what they say and we go from there.

Richard:

I would say that I plan pretty carefully – but I hardly ever end up teaching the plan – you teach people, not plans, so you have to be prepared to adjust things according to what comes up, or even abandon the plan completely.

17 Lesson planning: defining aims

A Warm-up

Choose the statement(s) you agree with. Then find a partner who has made similar choices to you, and agree on their order of importance.

Lesson aims are important because …
a   trainers (and directors of studies) require them
b   they make planning easier
c   they make lesson plans look more professional
d   they frame the criteria by which the lesson will be judged
e   learners need to know the focus of the lesson
f   they set a goal that can be used to test the learners' achievement.

B Types of aims

1   Work in pairs. Read the following six lesson aims. Five of them relate to the same lesson. Which is the odd one out?

a   To present and practise the form and use of the present perfect with *ever* and *never*.
b   By the end of the lesson the learners will have talked about and compared past experiences.
c   By the end of the lesson the learners will be able to express future plans and arrangements.
d   The learners will take part in informal conversation.
e   To develop my grammar presentation skills.
f   The lesson will help to build a good classroom dynamic.

2   Match aims a–f in activity B1 with the terms in the box.

communicative aim (x 2)   developmental aim   interpersonal aim   linguistic aim   skills aim

3   Choose the aim that best matches the teacher's description of her lesson below. What is unsatisfactory about the other aims?

a   to do some speaking
b   to present and practise the past tense
c   to practise writing
d   the learners will tell each other stories about disastrous holidays
e   to develop oral fluency when narrating past events
f   by the end of the lesson the learners will have learned some new words

I'm going to start by telling them about a recent holiday I had which was a bit of a disaster, and this will involve some past tense examples. Then I'm going to get them to work in pairs to reconstruct my story in writing, and I'll check that they've used the same verbs correctly. Then I'll ask them to think of their own stories, about trips or holidays where things went wrong, and to prepare to tell these stories to each other. To do this they'll first need to plan their stories, and I'll hand out dictionaries so they can look up any words they might need. Then I'll put them in pairs to tell their stories. Then I'll change the pairs so they can tell their stories again, to someone different. This way they can get more fluent, hopefully.

4 Read the lesson descriptions (A and B).

a Identify each teacher's main aims and at least one subsidiary aim.

b Formulate each teacher's aims (both main and subsidiary), using the rubric: *By the end of the lesson …*

Lesson A

I've got a short text about a driving instructor. So the students are going to read that and answer a couple of comprehension questions. I've chosen the text because there are lots of examples of the present perfect simple and continuous. So the text is a way of contextualising the language so that I can contrast the verb forms.

Lesson B

I've recorded two of my colleagues talking about their weekend, and I'm going to use this as a model for the learners to do the same thing, in pairs. There are one or two useful expressions in the recording, such as different ways of expressing evaluation: *not bad*, *pretty good*, *quite nice*, etc., so I'll want to focus on these at some point so that hopefully they will use them in the speaking activity.

Material and aims

1 For each of the following pieces of published material, identify and formulate:

a a main aim

b a possible subsidiary aim.

2 Classify the aims that you have formulated according to whether they are linguistic, communicative, or skills-focused.

BOAT ORDEAL BRITONS SURVIVE ON SEAWEED!

Family at sea for three days

A British family .....(1)..... **seaweed to stay alive as their boat** .....(2)..... **helplessly for three days on stormy seas.**

A two hour pleasure trip .....(3)..... a nightmare for Raymond Kearne, 48, his wife Jacqueline, 39, and seven-year-old son Jimmy, when their motorboat ran out of petrol. And all the time they .....(4)..... only 11 miles away from the crowded holiday beaches of Majorca. Raymond .....(5)..... yesterday at his villa on the island: 'We now know what it's like to face death – a horrible death at that.'

The family, who come from Lichfield, Staffs, ran out of fuel on their way back from a round-the-bay trip on Saturday.

Raymond said, 'The winds got very violent and .....(6)..... us out to sea.'

All that the family had taken with them was one bottle of orange juice.

Raymond said: 'On Monday, we were dying of thirst. We .....(7)..... filtering seawater so that we could drink it but it didn't work. So we .....(8)..... our own urine to save our lives. Then we ate seaweed. It .....(9)..... bloody awful.'

Just as they had given up hope, a Spanish fishing boat .....(10)..... and picked them up. The family were all suffering from sunburn, thirst and hunger.

Raymond used to have a pub on the holiday island but has now retired. He has put his boat up for sale.

'I didn't use to be afraid of the water, but I think I'll stay on dry land for a while,' he said.

| 6 | Speaking |

Discuss these questions with a partner.

1 Have you ever got on the wrong train or bus? When? What happened?
2 Have you ever had to take something back to a shop because there was something wrong with it? What was wrong with it?
3 When was the last time you called the wrong number by mistake?

Innovations (Pre-Intermediate) Dellar, Hocking and Walkley

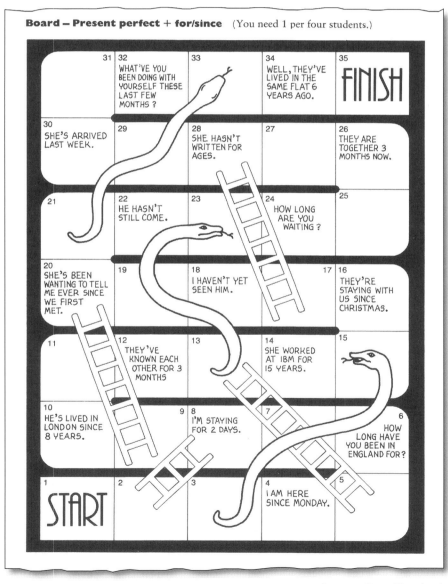

Board – Present perfect + for/since (You need 1 per four students.)

Grammar Games Rinvolucri

REFLECTION

Work in groups. Read these questions written by trainee teachers for their trainers.

a   Can you answer any of the trainees' questions?

b   If not, what further information would help you to give advice?

Andrew:

My lesson was meant to be about reading but the learners seemed to be enjoying the lead-in, the speaking activity, so much and they were all using English so I didn't want to stop them. But that meant that I didn't have much time for the reading. Do you think I should have finished the speaking activity sooner?

Sophie:

I started teaching and I thought the atmosphere was awful. The students seemed so bored. They had already done a long reading lesson before my lesson and there was no energy. I missed out some of the controlled practice of the new language because I just wanted to get to the game, which was more lively. I thought the lesson got better after that. Should I have done all the controlled practice? I know they were still making mistakes at the end.

Sam:

I don't find this elementary class very easy and wasn't very happy with that lesson. I wanted to teach language for talking about plans — but by the time I had explained 'going to' and the present continuous, and gone through how to make the sentences negative and how to make questions, the lesson was just about over and there was no time for any practice.

18 Alternative approaches to lesson design

A Warm-up

1 Complete the text, using the words *fluency* or *accuracy*.

> **Accuracy and fluency**
>
> By (1) .... we mean 'getting things right', and by (2) .... we mean 'getting your meaning across in real time'. In first language learning, (3) .... precedes (4) .... That is, we start by using our first language in order to convey our meanings, and only later do we achieve precision at doing this. But, in second language learning, the focus is traditionally on (5) .... first, and then (6) .... That is, language is presented and practised in isolated 'bits', and only when these can be produced correctly is the learner allowed to use them to express their personal meanings. There are alternative approaches to lesson design, however, that foreground (7) .... Learners are encouraged to express their personal meanings, and only later are these fine-tuned for (8) .... This type of approach is sometimes called a '(9) .... first' approach.

2 Work in pairs. Discuss the implications of the alternative approach suggested in the text.

B Two lesson designs

1 Work in pairs. Compare these two lesson designs. Describe their similarities and differences.

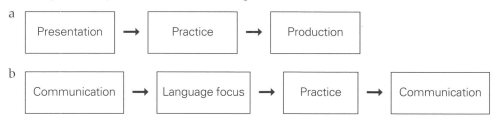

a

Presentation → Practice → Production

b

Communication → Language focus → Practice → Communication

2 Match this lesson description with one of the lesson designs in activity B1. Identify where each stage starts and finishes.

> We started off talking about families. I told the class about my family and then they told each other about theirs in groups. I then wrote 'I've got a *brother*' on the board and they told me words that could replace 'brother'. We practised the pronunciation too. We then did a little gap fill that focused on the difference between 'have' and 'has'. I then swapped the groups round and they told each other about their families again and this time the listeners tried to draw the family tree of the speaker.

3   Work in groups. Discuss these questions about the lesson in activity B2.

   a   What level is the class?
   b   Could the same lesson format work with a different level group?
   c   Why do you think the teacher swapped groups around for the final activity?
   d   What are some of the advantages of encouraging communication early in the lesson?
   e   Can you think of any disadvantages?

C   Task-based learning

One way of prioritising communication in the classroom is through 'task-based learning' (or 'activity-based learning'). Learners are given a task to do or a problem to solve. There is no prior focus on language. Only while they are doing the task, or immediately after its completion, are the learners given any explicit guidance as to the language items that might help them perform the task. They may then be given an opportunity to incorporate these items into a subsequent, similar, task.

1   Read the lesson outline and answer the questions.

> The teacher introduces the idea of 'the qualities of a good teacher'. Learners then work in small groups to produce a draft of a poster entitled 'Tips for teachers'. The teacher tells the learners that they will report back on what they have included and also give reasons for their choices. She gives them a few minutes to prepare and then the learners give their reports. The teacher puts a model sentence on the board and focuses on the form and meaning of 'should' to convey (mild) obligation and duty. The learners then complete sentences about other professions. For example: *A pilot shouldn't drink alcohol. A hairdresser should be friendly to clients.* The learners then work in groups to produce a poster entitled 'Tips for language learners'. The teacher later displays the posters on the wall.

   1   Can you identify a *communication → language focus → practice → communication* pattern?
   2   How could the teacher deal with the learners' immediate vocabulary needs?
   3   What happens after the learners produce a draft of their poster?
   4   Can you think of any advantages of ending the lesson with a similar task to the one used at the start?

2   Work in groups. Plan how to use the following task with an intermediate class.

   1   What vocabulary might be necessary for the successful completion of the task?
   2   What grammar patterns might the task create a need for?
   3   What would you anticipate including before the task?
   4   What do you think might be included after the task?

> You are the editors of a student magazine. You are planning to include a short article about the life of someone that you think will inspire your fellow students. You must decide together who you think would be a suitable subject. Afterwards you will report your discussion to the group and also the reasons for your final choice.

D Other lesson formats

1 Read the following activity and answer the questions.

Put the students into groups of five or six. Give each group a cassette/CD recorder. Their task is to make a recording for another group. They should record around five minutes but this may take up to 25 minutes as they use the pause and rewind buttons to rehearse, practise and correct what they say. When the recordings are made they should be exchanged with another group. The group then transcribes the recording they receive. These could be displayed on an overhead projector or photocopies can be made. The texts can then be analysed.

Adapted from *Dictation* Davis and Rinvolucri

1 Do you think this activity would work well with a class that you are currently teaching?
2 To what extent does this activity prioritise communication?
3 What skills are practised?
4 Identify the part of the lesson where the teacher may choose to focus on grammar and vocabulary.

2 Work in groups. Suggest how you could focus on the language areas that arise in these situations.

a A warm-up exercise generates a spontaneous discussion about an argument one learner had with a taxi driver. You notice that several learners need help expressing the idea of *shouldn't have done*. You decide to make a lesson point of this.
b At the beginning of a lesson a learner asks you how to make suggestions in English. You decide to present this language area and practise it.
c At the beginning of a lesson a learner asks what the difference is between 'taking an exam' and 'passing an exam'. You explain and also decide to expand this vocabulary field. You want to give a little practice and also provide an opportunity for communication.

REFLECTION

1 Work in groups. Read these contributions posted to an ELT discussion board. Suggest ideas that could help the teachers.

> **Felipe:** I get frustrated because I often present language at the start of the lesson and we practise it a lot, but the students hardly ever produce it in a freer situation at the end of the lesson.

> **Clare:** The coursebook I use is OK – but I always feel that the starting point is 'here is the grammar – what can you say with it?' rather than 'what do you want to say? – here's the grammar you need'.

> **Dave:** I'm quite newly qualified and I like the idea of using tasks in the lessons, particularly near the start of lessons, but I'm worried in case it throws up a language problem I can't explain.

> **Maria:** I've always tried to keep my lessons quite learner-centred. But when I teach grammar sometimes it seems inevitable that the lesson will be dominated by me, particularly at the start.

2 Think of your own teaching practice experience. Where have the substantial communication phases tended to come in lessons that you have taught?

19 Planning a scheme of work

Warm-up

Work in groups. Suggest how these complaints from learners could have been avoided.

Emiliano (from Italy):

> I used to like the lessons when I started but all we ever do is the coursebook. It's really boring now.

Eriko (from Japan):

> The teacher does new things with us every day but I can't remember everything about what we have done before.

Sophie (from France):

> I don't think all the things we do are useful. I wish the teacher would give us more chance to say what we want to do in lessons.

Thomas (from Germany):

> We have two teachers every morning. Before the break we did a long reading text and then after the break the next teacher did a reading lesson too. It was so boring.

Suriya (from Pakistan):

> I can't prepare for lessons because I never know what the teacher is going to do next. I find the class quite difficult and it would be better for me to do some work before the lesson.

B Schemes of work

Teachers are expected to plan their classes. We have already looked at plans for individual lessons and in this unit we are going to consider longer-term planning. A *scheme of work* (also sometimes called a *timetable*) is a plan which looks further ahead than just an individual lesson. Depending on the context in which they are working, teachers may be expected to produce a scheme of work for a week, a term, or even the entire year.

1   Work in pairs. Think back on the teaching practice lessons you have given or any lessons you have observed. Describe the characteristics of lessons where the main focus was on:

- grammar
- vocabulary
- social English (or functional English)
- receptive skills
- productive skills
- review
- exam preparation.

For example, were they more or less teacher-fronted? Was the pace urgent or relaxed?

B Classroom teaching

2 Work in pairs. Think back to your recent teaching practice sessions and answer the questions.

   a Over those sessions, have content, pace and interaction been well balanced?
   b If you have taught more than one level of class, in what ways were content, pace and interaction patterns different?

3 Consider the following teaching contexts. In what ways might a scheme of work differ in each context? Think about:

   • the balance of grammar vs skills lessons
   • the balance of receptive vs productive skills
   • the inclusion of social English lessons, of review lessons and of practice tests
   • the balance between teacher-fronted and learner-centred activities
   • the balance between intensive activities and more relaxed activities.

   a A group of 12 elementary learners studying two evenings a week for nine months in their home country.
   b A group of 18 intermediate learners studying three hours a day for a month in a private language school in the UK.
   c A group of 15 upper-intermediate learners in New Zealand preparing for the IELTS exam, a good result in which will give them access to university study; they have two months of classes, studying 20 hours a week.
   d A one-to-one class for an advanced student of business English, that takes place three hours a day, for two weeks, in central London.
   e A group of migrant workers and refugees studying in Canada; they have two three-hour lessons a week for thirty weeks. None of the class is above CEF level A1 and some have additional literacy needs.

C Sequencing lessons

Read the timetable and answer the questions.

Level: intermediate
Number of lessons: three lessons per day, three days per week
Type of course: general English, focus on language skills and language systems

	Monday	Wednesday	Friday
09 – 9.50	Grammar – uses of 'should' and 'must'	Speaking – roleplay – job interviews	Functional language – asking for advice
10 – 10.50	Listening – working in a call centre	Speaking and writing – preparing a news story	Speaking – jobs
11 – 11.50	Grammar revision – present perfect simple	Reading – how to do well in a job interview	Vocabulary – collocations with 'make'

1 In terms of quantity in the week, is there a reasonable balance between vocabulary, grammar and skills work?
2 Is there a reasonable balance of lesson types on each day?
3 Are there obvious links between the lessons that are planned for the week?

84

D Lesson planning game

Work in groups. Use the cards your trainer gives you to plan the lessons for the week. Then compare ideas with another group.

	Monday	Tuesday	Wednesday	Thursday	Friday
09–09.50					
10–10.50					
11–11.50					
12– 12.50					

REFLECTION

Work as a group. Plan a sequence of lessons based on the coursebook that you are using in teaching practice. Your trainer will tell you how many lessons you should plan.

- Ensure that there is a variety of types of lesson.
- You can use additional material to that in your coursebook if you wish.

20 Motivating learners

A Warm-up

1 Look at the list of factors that may influence a learner's attitude to their language learning. Divide the list into two groups. Compare ideas with a partner. What criteria did you use to divide the factors?

Factors that may influence a learner's attitude to their language learning:
- The learner finds the material interesting.
- The learner knows that a good level of English will benefit their career.
- The learner really likes English literature and wants to read it in the original language.
- The teacher praises and encourages learners.
- The learner likes socialising with the other members of the class.
- The learner feels the lessons are useful.

2 Work in groups. Think about a learner from one of your teaching practice classes who appears 'highly motivated'.

1 How is this motivation demonstrated?
2 Can you suggest reasons for their level of motivation?

B Things teachers can influence

1 Work in pairs. Discuss the following questions.

1 Do you think the teacher should set targets that are easy to achieve, difficult to achieve, or somewhere in-between?
2 Do you think learners respond best to having a set routine in lessons, a routine which is occasionally broken, or lots and lots of variety?
3 Do you think learners respond better to cooperative or to competitive games?
4 Do you think that all learners can be motivated using the same strategies?

2 Read the text and decide how the authors would answer the questions in activity B1.

Motivation in the classroom setting

In a teacher's mind, motivated students are usually those who participate actively in the class, express interest in the subject matter and study a great deal. Teachers can easily recognise characteristics such as these. They also have more opportunity to influence these characteristics than students' reasons for studying the second language or their attitudes towards the language and its speakers. If we can make our classrooms places where the students enjoy coming because the content is interesting and relevant to their age and level of ability, where the learning goals are challenging yet manageable and clear, and where the atmosphere is supportive and non-threatening, we can make a positive contribution to the students' motivation to learn.

Although little research has been done to investigate how pedagogy interacts with motivation in second language classrooms, considerable work has been done within the field of educational psychology.

In a review of this work Graham Crookes and Richard Schmidt (1991)[1] point to several areas where educational research has reported increased levels of motivation for students in relation to pedagogical practices. Included among these are:

Motivating students into the lesson At the opening stages of lessons (and within transitions), it has been observed that remarks teachers make about forthcoming activities can lead to higher levels of interest on the part of the students.

Varying the activities, tasks and materials Students are reassured by the existence of classroom routines which they can depend on. However, lessons which always consist of the same routines, patterns and formats have been shown to lead to a decrease in attention and an increase in boredom. Varying the activities, tasks and materials can help to avoid this and increase students' interest levels.

Using co-operative rather than competitive goals Co-operative learning activities are those in which students must work together in order to complete a task or solve a problem. These techniques have been found to increase the self-confidence of students, including weaker ones, because every participant in a co-operative task has an important role to play. Knowing that their team-mates are counting on them can increase students' motivation.

Clearly, cultural and age differences will determine the most appropriate way for teachers to motivate students. In some classrooms, students may thrive on competitive interaction, while in others, co-operative activities will be more successful.

[1] Crookes, G. & Schmidt, R. (1991) 'Motivation: Reopening the research agenda' Language Learning 41/4:469–512

How Languages are Learned Lightbown and Spada

3 Read the text again and answer the questions.

1 Can a teacher influence a learner's motives for learning a language?
2 Are the points made based on ELT research or more general educational studies?
3 Are the points applicable to an ELT classroom?
4 What two factors do the authors identify as impacting on how teachers could try to motivate learners?
5 Think back to a recent teaching practice session.
   - Were learners 'motivated into the lesson'?
   - Were activities, tasks and materials varied?
   - Were tasks largely cooperative or competitive?

C Ways of influencing motivation

Read the following comments made by learners and teachers and answer the questions.

1 Which things that are mentioned could you realistically do in teaching practice on this course?
2 Which things do you think you could do if you had your own class for a fairly long period of time?
3 Which things will influence motivation for a short period of time (during one lesson)?
4 Which things will influence motivation over a longer period of time?

B Classroom teaching

Learners' views

a Fan Kong:

I don't like it when I do a bit of homework and then don't get it back for a long time. It really annoys me. I think teachers should **give work back quickly**.

b Erica:

I remember when I was thinking my English would never get better and my teacher always told me it would and always said how well I was doing. It made me feel better – I think teachers should **encourage students** as much as they can – it's really important.

c Lewis:

One of the lessons I like best is when the teacher tells us to choose a reading from the internet – anything we like. And then we write some questions and give them to another student and they answer them. It's fun for **students to choose the material** sometimes.

d Sonham:

I think it is really important for the teachers to give us **tests** sometimes. It makes me look back at work we've done before and makes me realise how much I have learned.

e Suzanna:

I remember a course where all the lessons were too easy for me – it was terrible – I didn't learn anything. But my friend, he said he went to a class and told me it was too difficult and he stopped going. It's important that teachers **make it the right level**.

Teachers' views

a Jason:

I sometimes get learners to make posters and things and it's always nice if you **put work on the walls** so everyone can see it. I even do it with essays and things sometimes because at least then there is some sort of readership and audience created.

b Bhupendra:

I think it's important to **set objectives** for students – make sure they know what's expected of them. Sometimes I give them a list of things that I think they should be able to do by the end of term or something like that – make a simple telephone call in English – that kind of thing – and get them to tick them off as they think they achieve them.

c Lucy:

I set objectives, but I speak to each learner individually – after every ten hours or so of lessons – and discuss what they want to achieve and how they will do it. **Personalised, achievable objectives** really help to motivate learners, I think.

d Paige:

I often **ask learners about what they want to do** – and also what sort of lessons they like. This way it's much easier to meet their needs and that always makes them more motivated.

e Naomi:

> We use a coursebook quite a lot but it can get a little repetitive so every few lessons I try to do something very different. We have a project, like make a class newspaper, or I record some adverts and do some worksheets to go with them or something like that. **Variety** is so important, I think.

D Adapting material

One factor that may influence motivation in the classroom is the intrinsic interest generated by the material. Activities do not always need to be adapted but a teacher may sometimes choose to try to make an activity more interesting.

1 Read the following exercise and the teacher's explanation of how and why he adapted it.

1 What has the teacher done to make the activity more motivating?
2 Can you think of any other ways of adapting the original material?

Complete the sentences. Use one word only.

1 He's not very good .... singing.
2 Did you pay .... those sweets?
3 You should apologise .... her immediately.
4 When I get the answer wrong the teacher always shouts .... me.
5 Who do you agree .... ? Me or Bob?
6 I must be in love. I think .... her all the time.
7 Did you know that Paula is afraid .... mice?
8 Don't worry. Just explain .... Mary how you feel.

'It was a useful enough exercise but we had done quite a lot of gap filling stuff just before and I thought it would be good to change the pace of the lesson a bit. Instead, I just wrote the words 'good', 'pay', 'apologise' and so on out several times on little bits of paper and put them in a bag. The students then had to take two or three of the words and write true sentences about themselves using the words. 'I'm afraid of dogs', 'I sometimes don't agree with my boss' – that kind of thing. They then compared what they had written.'

---

2 Suggest ways to make the following task more motivating.

Choose a person you have read about, or learned about, in your coursebook. Describe the character to your classmate. Can they guess who it is?

---

3 Work in pairs. Think of an activity you have done in your teaching practice lessons that could have been made more interesting. How could it have been adapted?

B Classroom teaching

REFLECTION

1 Answer the questions and write the answers in the grid.

1 If learners start to get disheartened it helps for the teacher to .... – so they can see how far they have come. (4 & 8 letters)

2 One way of achieving 1, is to give learners short ....(5 letters)

3 We all do better if we hear a bit of this from time to time. (13 letters)

4 A combination of different things gives .... (7 letters)

5 If teachers do this, then not only might learners be more motivated but the room might look nice too! (7 & 4 letters)

6 In order to .... of the learners, teachers can ask what they like doing and what they want to do. (4, 3 and 5 letters)

7 These may be cooperative or competitive, and are usually fun in the classroom. (5 letters)

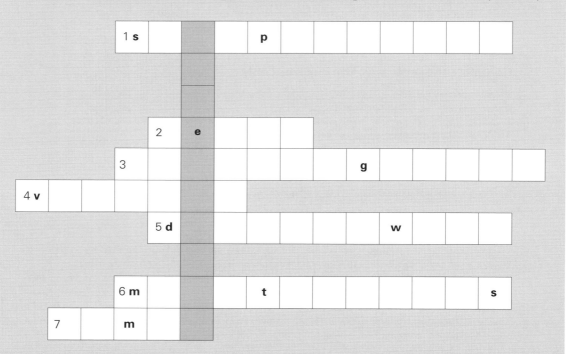

2 When you have finished, complete the word in the grey block and write an appropriate clue for it.

90

21 Teaching different levels

A Warm-up

1 Read these descriptions of learner proficiency and answer the questions.

   a Which one describes the highest level?

   b Which one describes the lowest level?

Can interact with a degree of fluency and spontaneity that makes regular interaction with native speakers quite possible without strain for either party. Can produce clear, detailed text on a wide range of subjects and explain a viewpoint on a topical issue giving the advantages and disadvantages of different options.	
Can understand and use familiar everyday expressions and very basic phrases aimed at the satisfaction of needs of a concrete type [...] Can interact in a simple way provided the other person talks slowly and clearly and is prepared to help.	
Can express him/herself fluently and spontaneously without much obvious searching for expressions. Can use language flexibly and effectively for social, academic and professional purposes. Can produce clear, well-structured, detailed text on complex subjects.	
Can understand sentences and frequently used expressions related to areas of most immediate relevance [...] Can communicate in simple and routine tasks requiring a simple and direct exchange of information on familiar and routine matters.	
Can deal with most situations likely to arise whilst traveling in an area where the language is spoken. Can produce simple connected text on topics which are familiar or of personal interest. Can describe experiences and events, dreams, hopes and ambitions and briefly give reasons and explanations for opinions and plans.	

Common European Framework of Reference for Languages Council of Europe

2 Read the text about the Common European Framework and label the descriptors in the table above.

> **The Common European Framework**
>
> The *Common European Framework of Reference for Languages* (CEF) is a 'detailed model for describing and scaling language use'. It provides descriptors of learners at three broad levels: A: *basic user*; B: *independent user*; and C: *proficient user*. Each level is divided into two bands: A1, A2; B1, B2; C1, C2. The descriptors in the table represent levels C1, B2, B1, A2 and A1.

3 Use these descriptors to rate your own ability in a second (or third, etc.) language. Compare answers with a partner.

4 Complete these sentences in any way that seems appropriate to you. Then compare ideas with a partner.

   a At higher levels learners might need ....

   b At lower levels learners might need ....

   c I like teaching .... level learners because ....

B Classroom teaching

B Adapting to different levels

1 Match these comments with the CELTA trainees who made them.

Rachel moved from teaching an elementary class (i.e. CEF A2) to teaching an upper-intermediate class (i.e. CEF B2).

Tom moved from teaching an upper-intermediate class to teaching an elementary class.

a

In the other group I didn't mind if the learners used their own language a bit – but I try to stop it completely now.

b

I realise that the learners I have now can already say a lot of what they want to and my job is partly to give them alternative ways of saying things.

c

I got a real shock when I started with this new group. I don't think they understood anything I said in the first lesson! There was an exercise that was quite easy but I just couldn't get across what they had to do.

d

I thought I wouldn't be able to use authentic material with this group, but I found a menu that was quite easy and we had a really good lesson on food vocabulary.

e

I've noticed that I have more activities in a lesson and they tend to be a bit shorter – particularly pair- and groupwork doesn't last as long.

f

I really have to work hard to research grammar now. The learners sometimes ask quite difficult questions and so I really work hard before the lesson.

g

I can't just chat to this group and find out about them as people so easily. I don't think I have such a good rapport with them.

2 Work in pairs. Compare your experiences.

    a If you have not yet taught at different levels, who do you think you can learn more from, Rachel or Tom?

    b If you have already taught at different levels, have your experiences been similar?

C Productive skills

1 Work in pairs. Read this speaking activity and answer the questions.

    1 What do the learners do before they speak?

    2 Can you predict the sort of exchanges that would happen in part 3?

Speak out

1 Write five questions about clothes and shopping for clothes. Use one or more of the words below in each question.
What do you *like* *wearing* in the *evenings*?

2 Answer your own questions on a piece of paper.

3 Ask other students your questions. Whose answers are the most similar to yours?

Clockwise (Elementary) Potten and Potten

2 Work in groups. Discuss how you would expect a more advanced speaking activity to be different.

Now read the following activity. Are the activities different in the ways you predicted?

Speak out

In groups of three, **A**, **B**, and **C**, toss a coin to play the game. **A** talk about recent activities, **B** ask questions, and **C** monitor. Swap roles.

1 food and drink	2 concerts and plays	3 family and friends	4 study	5 travel
START ☞				
12 cars		1 square — HEADS / TAILS — 2 squares		6 work
11 housework	10 letters	9 sports	8 TV	7 books

Clockwise (Advanced) Jeffries

3 How would you expect writing tasks to differ between lower and higher levels?

D Receptive skills

1 Read the following listening transcript. What level do you think it would be appropriate for: elementary, intermediate, or advanced? Why?

> Well, it was something I had talked about wanting to do for quite a while and then when my boyfriend gave it to me as a birthday present last April I think I was more shocked than anything. I would actually have to do it. On the day I woke up terrified. At first I refused to go but then my boyfriend said how marvellous it was so we drove out to Kawarau bridge which is just over 20 kms from my home in Queenstown, New Zealand. Everything was ready and I got careful instructions for what to do. Standing on the edge of the bridge I had a real sense that 'this was it' and I suppose my life did pass before my eyes! Then I jumped ... and it was all over so fast, and there I was bouncing about at the end of this rope just a few metres above the river. Unbelievable ... I can quite honestly say it was a once in a lifetime experience.

Choice Mohamed and Aklam

2 Read how three teachers used this listening text at different levels. Match the descriptions with the levels: elementary, intermediate and advanced.

a
> 'I played the first sentence "cold" and asked them to predict what "it" referred to. I carried on like that, playing little chunks at a time, until they got it.'

b
> 'I put up three pictures of different adventure sports: hang-gliding, scuba diving and bungee jumping. I elicited the kinds of places you do these sports (e.g. in the mountains, in the sea, off a bridge). Then I told them that they were going to listen to someone describing their first-time experience with one of these sports. They had to listen and choose which one. I played the recording two or three times, stopping at strategic points, and let them discuss the task in pairs between each playing. I then handed out the transcript.'

c
> 'I dictated the following questions:
> 1 What adventure sport is the woman describing?   3 Where did she go to do it?
> 2 How did she feel beforehand?   4 How did she feel afterwards?
> Then I played the recording, checked the answers and re-played the bits they were having trouble with. I played the recording another couple of times and each time set some more questions before listening. Then we talked about adventure sports they had done, or would like to do.'

3 Work in groups. Discuss what these tasks suggest about dealing with listening texts at different levels.

E Teaching grammar

1 Work in groups. Discuss how you would expect grammar input to differ between levels. Consider:
- the way in which a context is created
- how much is taught
- the complexity of the rules that are given
- the type of practice activities that are used

2 Work in groups. Discuss the aspects of grammar input that you would expect to remain the same at different levels.

3 Compare these two coursebook extracts.

1 In what ways are the extracts similar?
2 In what ways are the extracts different?
3 How accurate were your predictions in Activities E1 and E2?

Present perfect simple & continuous

1 Look at the verbs in these pairs of sentences from the Lara Croft interview. Answer the questions below.

Pair A
They**'ve been** a bit frosty since I started the job.
I**'ve had** my trusty old Land Rover for years.

Pair B
He**'s tried** to climb Everest three times.
He**'s just written** a book.

Pair C
I**'ve been doing** this job since I was 21.
I **haven't been seeing** anyone recently.

Verb structure?
a) What is the name of the verb structure used in each pair of sentences?

Dynamic or stative?
b) Which two pairs of sentences have verbs with dynamic meanings?
c) Which pair of sentences has verbs with stative meanings?

Complete or incomplete?
d) Which pair of sentences shows actions that are complete?
e) Which pair of sentences shows situations that are incomplete or ongoing?
f) Which pair of sentences shows actions that are incomplete or ongoing?

2 Match the beginnings (a–d) with the endings (1–4) to make four important rules about the use of the present perfect simple and continuous.

a) Verb with dynamic meaning + the present perfect simple:
b) Verb with stative meaning + the present perfect simple:
c) Verb with dynamic meaning + the present perfect continuous:
d) Verb with stative meaning + the present perfect continuous:

1 the action is incomplete or ongoing.   3 not usually used.
2 the action is complete.   4 the situation is incomplete or ongoing.

3 Work with a partner. Choose the most appropriate form of the present perfect, and then ask each other the questions.

a) How long **have you saved / have you been saving** with the same bank?
b) **Have you ever broken / Have you ever been breaking** your arm or your leg?
c) How long **have you had / have you been having** your current e-mail address?
d) **Have you ever been / Have you ever been going** to Berlin?
e) How long **have you driven / have you been driving** the same car?
f) **Have you ever missed / Have you ever been missing** a plane?
g) **Have you ever eaten / Have you ever been eating** oysters?
h) How many times **have you taken / have you been taking** English exams?
i) How long **have you known / have you been knowing** your English teacher?
j) How many times **have you done / have you been doing** exercises on the present perfect?

Inside Out (Upper-Intermediate) Kay and Jones

B Classroom teaching

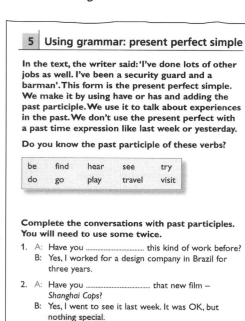

5 | Using grammar: present perfect simple

In the text, the writer said: 'I've done lots of other jobs as well. I've been a security guard and a barman'. This form is the present perfect simple. We make it by using have or has and adding the past participle. We use it to talk about experiences in the past. We don't use the present perfect with a past time expression like last week or yesterday.

Do you know the past participle of these verbs?

be	find	hear	see	try
do	go	play	travel	visit

Complete the conversations with past participles. You will need to use some twice.

1. A: Have you .... this kind of work before?
   B: Yes, I worked for a design company in Brazil for three years.

2. A: Have you .... that new film – *Shanghai Cops*?
   B: Yes, I went to see it last week. It was OK, but nothing special.

3. A: Have you .... from Jing recently?
   B: Yes, she rang me a few days ago actually, and guess what? She's .... a new job with a much bigger company. We're going out next week to celebrate.

4. A: Have you .... our country before?
   B: No, this is the first time I've ever .... here.

5. A: We're going to a Vietnamese restaurant tonight. Would you like to come with us?
   B: Yes, I'd love to. I've never .... Vietnamese food before.

6. A: Have you .... this game before? You're very good at it.
   B: No, never, but I have .... something similar.

7. A: Have you .... round Asia much?
   B: Yes, I have, actually. I've .... to Singapore, Thailand, the Philippines, Japan. Quite a few places, really.

Did you notice the answers in sentences 1–3? We often use the past simple to give details about when our past experiences happened.

With a partner, practise the conversations.

6 | Practice

Put the words in order and make questions.

1. much / you / have / travelled
   .... ?

2. much / food / foreign / you / tried / have
   .... ?

3. any / films / recently / you / seen / have / good
   .... ?

4. CDs / bought / any / you / good / recently / have
   .... ?

5. many / before / you / had / have / jobs
   .... ?

6. this / grammar / before / you / studied / have
   .... ?

Now ask a partner the questions. Try to answer as in the conversations in Activity 5.

Innovations (Pre-Intermediate) Dellar, Hocking and Walkley

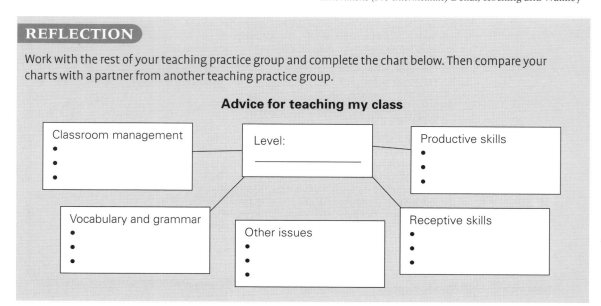

REFLECTION

Work with the rest of your teaching practice group and complete the chart below. Then compare your charts with a partner from another teaching practice group.

Advice for teaching my class

Classroom management
-
-
-

Level:
_____

Productive skills
-
-
-

Vocabulary and grammar
-
-
-

Other issues
-
-
-
-

Receptive skills
-
-
-

22 English for Special Purposes

A Warm-up

Talk to as many people as possible. Ask questions to find someone who:

* has a degree in a science subject
* has worked in business
* has worked in journalism
* has written an academic essay of at least 9000 words
* has presented a paper at a conference
* subscribes to a specialist journal or magazine
* has designed a web page
* has taught a school subject that is not a language

How many of your colleagues have specialist knowledge of some sort?

B Special purposes

1 Put these learners and classes in the correct columns.

English for Special (or Specific) Purposes (ESP)	General English

a A Japanese marine biologist is preparing to present a research paper in English at an international conference.
b An intermediate class of young adults of different nationalities are preparing to sit the Cambridge First Certificate in English examination.
c A group of French air traffic controllers are receiving instruction in aviation English.
d An Argentinean civil rights activist is planning a trip to an international conference, and wants to brush up her social English skills.
e A Croatian businessman, who lives and works in Croatia, has to handle regular email and phone communication in English, and occasionally take part in conference calls in English.
f A group of students from China are getting instruction in how to write academic essays in English, in preparation for post-graduate study at a university in New Zealand.
g Workers and clerical staff attend an on-site beginners level English class at a paint factory in Poland.

2 Work in pairs. Answer the questions.

1 In which of the ESP situations would the teacher need to have extensive specialist knowledge in the learner's/learners' subject area?
2 Which of the above situations are one-to-one teaching situations, as opposed to group ones?

C Needs analysis

The first stage in designing an ESP course is usually to conduct a *needs analysis*, i.e. an assessment of the specific needs of the learners. This is usually done by means of questionnaires and interviews.

Work in groups. Read the requirements and decide what information you would need in order to prepare for the course. Think of at least six questions to ask the learners about their job-specific English needs.

> The local port authority needs a language course for a group of marine safety inspectors. Their job involves carrying out safety inspections on visiting ships. These inspections are conducted and reported on in English.

D Text analysis

People who work or study together typically share the same way of using language. They belong to a special *discourse community*. In designing and teaching an ESP course, it is important to understand the discourse conventions of the target community. This involves studying the kinds of language and texts that the members of the discourse community use and produce.

1 Read this extract from an official online manual for marine safety inspectors. What special features of the vocabulary and grammar do you notice?

The inspector shall thoroughly check the watertight door systems to verify that they are in satisfactory operating condition. The enclosures for all local control door switches and controllers should be examined for evidence of water or corrosion. It has been found that faulty operation of electrically operated watertight doors may be caused by seawater entering the local control switch located at the watertight door. If seawater has entered the switch enclosure, it may short circuit the motor starter and motor so that the door opens even with the wheelhouse control indicating the 'closed' position. To the extent practical, the inspector shall also be satisfied that the ship's personnel are familiar with the watertight door system, location of disconnect switches, etc.

(from USCG Marine Safety Manual, Vol. II)

2 Here are some examples of entries made by inspectors when making their reports. Comment on the vocabulary and grammar in these texts.

OFFICIAL REPORTS

a Examined all pressure/vacuum valves and flame screens after they were opened for inspection; all were found satisfactory with the exception of those noted on page 6.
b All items listed on pages 4 through 7 were inspected and found satisfactory except as noted.
c Visited vessel to inspect progress of construction of the hull and internal structural members. All work was proceeding satisfactorily in accordance with approved plans. Several areas in the port fuel tank were marked for pickup welding.
d A final inspection of the vessel's entire underwater body was made prior to launching and found satisfactory. Initial drydock examination completed.

(from USCG Marine Safety Manual, Vol. II)

3   Write questions an inspector needs to ask in order to produce statements like the ones in activity D2.

4   Work in groups. Suggest some classroom tasks appropriate for a group of marine safety inspectors who need to use English.

E   Materials

Read the extract from an ESP course and answer the questions.

1   What is the 'special purpose' for this course?
2   How does the material differ from a general English course?
3   How is the material similar to a general English course?

The words you need ... to talk about change

1   Match the sentences with the sales trends (a–e).

1 Sales went up a lot last month.
2 Sales have fallen gradually this year.
3 Turnover increased a little but then went down by €2 million.
4 Market share has stayed the same for the last few years.
5 Turnover decreased in the first quarter but went up by the end of the year.

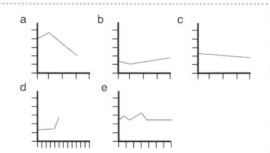

2   The tenses we use with the language of trends are very important.

Past years/months

We use the past simple: *Sales went up last month / last year / in January.*

Current year

If the year is not finished, we use the present perfect: *Sales have gone up this year.*

Complete the sentences with the correct form of the verb given.

1 Unemployment .... (decrease) by 5% last year.
2 Inflation .... (rise) by 2% so far this year.
3 Bank interest rates .... (fall) by 0.5% last month.
4 Taxes .... (increase) a lot already this year.
5 Petrol prices .... (go up) by 20 cents in July.

It's time to talk

We can describe increases and decreases like this:

	Subject	Up/down	How big	When
Past simple	Sales	decreased	a little	last year.
Present perfect	Business/Sales	has/have increased	a lot	this year.

Now work with a partner and use the table to help you describe important changes in:

• your organisation last year
• your country.

Were the changes good or bad?

English 365 Dignen, Flinders and Sweeney

F One-to-one

1 Work in pairs. Discuss the advantages and disadvantages of teaching one-to-one. Consider:
- syllabus
- materials
- activities
- interaction
- motivation

2 Suggest ways to counter some of the negative factors you identified in activity F1.

G Assessment

1 Assessment of ESP students often involves identifying and testing specific *competencies*. These often take the form of '*can do*' statements. Put these statements in order, from beginners to advanced.

Work-related 'can do' statements for the skills of listening and speaking.

a Can offer advice to clients within own job area or simple matters.

b Can contribute effectively to meetings and seminars within own area of work and argue for or against a case.

c Can take and pass on simple messages of a routine kind, such as 'Friday meeting 10 a.m.'

d Can advise on / handle complex delicate or contentious issues, such as legal or financial matters, to the extent that he / she has the necessary specialist knowledge.

e Can take and pass on most messages that are likely to require attention during a normal working day.

f Can state simple requirements within own job area, such as 'I want to order 25 of …'.

(adapted from *Common European Framework of Reference for Languages: Learning, teaching, assessment* Council of Europe)

2 Suggest how you would test the following competency.

Can take and pass on most messages that are likely to require attention during a normal working day.

REFLECTION

1 Work in groups. How far do you agree with these statements?
a Teaching ESP is more satisfying than teaching general English, because you have a much better idea of your learners' needs.
b Teaching ESP requires not only knowledge of English, but also knowledge of the subject area of your learners.
c Learners need a basic grounding in general English before they can start learning ESP.
d *All* English language learners are really ESP learners.

2 Think about your own interests and specialisms. Could *you* offer an ESP course?

23 Teaching literacy

A Warm-up

Read the definition of literacy and answer the questions.

> 'Literacy is the ability to read and write in a language, usually one's own. However, increasingly learners of a second language, especially those living in an English as a second language (ESL) context, require native–like literacy skills in order to function effectively in the target culture. In other words, they need to achieve *functional literacy*… simply 'doing reading and writing' in class is unlikely to meet the specific needs of such learners.'

An A–Z of ELT Thornbury

1 What typical reading and writing challenges face a new arrival to the UK (or Australia, or Canada)? For example, understanding, and filling in, a national insurance application form.
2 Why is 'doing reading and writing' in class unlikely to meet the special needs of such learners?

B L1 and L2 literacy

Read the learner profiles and answer the questions.

> Aasmah moved to the UK from Afghanistan nearly three years ago. She has picked up a fair amount of spoken language but has never had formal lessons. She cannot read or write any English but has a good command of writing in Farsi, her native language.
>
> Halima moved to the UK from Somalia. She works in the UK and listens and speaks well. However, she cannot read or write any English and she never had the opportunity to learn to read or write in her own language either.
>
> Huseyin is an electronics engineer and a recent arrival in the UK from Iraq. He is literate in both Kurdish and Arabic, and speaks English fluently. He can read and write English sentences but cannot handle the kinds of documents that he needs in order to apply for a job, rent a flat, or get a driving licence, for example.

1 To what extent is each one literate or illiterate in a) their first language(s); b) English?
2 Why would it be difficult to comment on the overall level of English possessed by both Aasmah and Halima?
3 Consider the ways in which most learners are taught new vocabulary and grammar. Why might Aasmah and Halima find learning these things harder than some classmates?
4 What skills, if any, do you think Aasmah may be able to transfer from reading and writing in Farsi to reading and writing in English?
5 Why do you think that the ability to read and write sentences is insufficient for Huseyin's needs?
6 What else does he need to know about reading and writing in order to achieve 'functional literacy'?

C Lessons from learners

Read what these learners say about learning to read and/or write in English. In each case write what you should remember when you teach basic literacy. Then compare your answers with a partner.

Learner	Comment	I should remember ...
Karim	I always got very anxious before reading things in class. It's quite intimidating. It helps if there is not too much on the page and if the writing is quite big.	
Soula	I was very lucky with my teacher. She gave me lots of time. And sometimes I read with an assistant teacher. They never got frustrated with me and always encouraged me.	
Li Na	It was a bit frustrating. The teacher kept practising letters and sounds. Eventually we went on to words. And then sentences. It was months before I read a little story. I wanted to move on.	
Shireen	It's very frustrating if you are trying to learn to read but you don't actually understand the words anyway – they are all new.	
Ali	The worst thing is that it is just so tiring. I concentrate so much I get tired and then my writing gets worse.	
Samia	My teacher always said 'copy this from the board' – new words, grammar, those things – but I never had time. I felt I missed out and fell behind the other students.	
Hussein	My handwriting was very bad – the teacher couldn't read what I was writing. I found it so difficult. But then a teacher helped me and showed me how to hold the pen and now I'm improving a little.	
Mei Yan	Some people in my class can read and write quite well. They write quickly but for me, if I copy things, I can't remember more than one or two letters at a time. It's very difficult.	

D Reading activities

Work in pairs. Put these reading activities into the correct column.

Activities focusing on reading at word level	Activities focusing on reading at sentence level	Activities focusing on reading at text level

a Reading Bingo
   The teacher gives out bingo cards with known vocabulary on them. She reads out items of vocabulary and the winner is the first person to tick off all the words.

b Find and underline
   The teacher gives out a short text about eating habits. The learners must underline all the types of food mentioned.

c Odd one out
   The teacher writes words on the board and the learners have to say which word is the odd one out. For example, *March*, *April*, <u>*Tuesday*</u>, *June*.

d Matching
   The teacher gives out pictures of known vocabulary, and the corresponding words on pieces of card. The learners must match the pictures to the appropriate word.

e Ordering
   The teacher gives out a short text but the sentences are in the wrong order. The learners must put the text into the correct order.

f Describing pictures
   Learners read a series of sentences and choose the correct picture in each case. For example, there are two pictures, one of a set of keys on a table, and one with keys on a chair. The learners read 'My keys are on the table' and must select the correct picture.

g Next word
   The teacher gives out a short text. The teacher begins to read the text to the class, but every now and then stops and asks, 'What is the next word?'

E Writing activities

Identify three writing sub-skills and find two activities that practise each one in the following activities.

a The teacher gives out a handout on which there are pictures of known vocabulary. Scattered around the picture are the letters to make the written form and a space underneath for the form to be written.

b There are letters of the alphabet on a piece of paper. But the letters are in the form of a series of dots and the learners must join the dots to form the letters.

c The learners are given a sentence and under the sentence is a space for them to write their own, with the first word given. The learners must write a similar sentence.

   Ania is from Poland.
   I ....

d The teacher gives out a series of pictures which represent simple sentences. The learners must write the sentences.

e The teacher writes simple words on pieces of paper in thick board pen. She gives one to each learner. The learners place another piece of paper over this and then trace the word onto their own piece of paper.

f The teacher selects eight items of vocabulary each week and teaches the written form. Every day the learners must read the words, and then cover them and try to write them out correctly.

F Functional literacy

1 Read the coursebook extract. Explain how the writing activities are similar to or different from those in General English courses.

A coursebook targeted at developing functional literacy for recent arrivals in Australia

Writing a formal letter of complaint

George writes this letter to the real estate agent after his phone call.

1 Skim the letter to get an idea of the topic. What is the letter about?

_____

2/96 Beach Street
Emerald 2026
1 June

Dear Sir / Madam:

I am writing about the stove in our flat. Two elements are not working and the thermostat in the oven does not appear to be working accurately either. As you can appreciate, with only two elements functioning and the oven out of order it is extremely difficult to prepare a meal for a family of five.

I have already rung and reported this problem twice (14th of May and the 21st of May) but nothing has been done about it yet.

This problem is urgent therefore I would appreciate it if you could arrange to have an electrician come and fix the stove immediately.

Yours sincerely,

1. George Wim
George Win

1. Closing
2. Writer's signature and name
3. Justification of complaint
4. Writer's address
5. Date
6. Request for action
7. Greetings
8. Identification of complaint

2 Check the meaning of any unknown words in your dictionary or ask your teacher. Then read the letter.

3 Read the list of functions 1 to 8 on the right of George's letter. Write a number next to the parts of the letter which match these functions. The first one has been done for you.

4 Read the letter again and answer the questions.
a. What is George complaining about?
   _____

b. What justification does George give for his complaint?
   _____

c. What action does George want the agent to take?
   _____

5 Think of an issue that you have wanted to complain about recently.

  a. Decide which authority you will need to send your letter to. Will it be the local council, a real estate agent, a company, the local school or the Environmental Protection Authority?

  _____

  b. Find out the name of the person in that organisation that you will need to send your letter to.

  _____

6 Make notes on this sheet before you write your letter.

  Subject of the letter _____

  Content of the letter (in note form)_____

  Problem _____

  Details _____

  Action requested _____

  Closing phrases _____

  Yours _____

7 Write a draft of your letter. Use some of these expressions to help you with your draft.

I am writing to complain about the I am writing about the I am writing to you regarding the		stove plumbing noise from the nearby factory neighbour's barking dog
As you can appreciate As a result Consequently	it is difficult to	prepare a meal have a shower sleep study
Therefore	I would appreciate it if you could I would be grateful if you could	arrange to have someone look at it. get a plumber to come and fix it. organise someone to check this. contact the owner and …

8 Discuss your draft with other students in the class and your teacher. Then write a final draft. Show you final draft to your teacher.

Beach Street Delaruelle

2 Work in pairs. Suggest other types of text that new arrivals in an English-speaking country would need to master, and which would lend themselves to the same approach.

REFLECTION

Work in groups. Complete the diagram below.

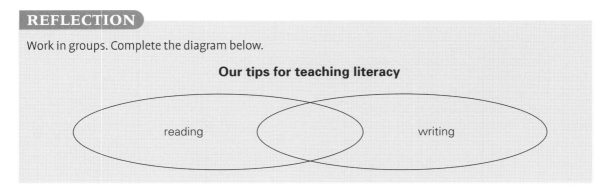

Our tips for teaching literacy

reading   writing

24 Monitoring and assessing learning

A Warm-up

Answer as many questions as you can in five minutes.

Revision test
1 How is the future continuous formed?
2 Which form is best, and why?
   a Ah, where's my diary? Oh, yes, here it is. I thought so, *I'm meeting / I'll meet* Laura on the 14th.
   b People *will buy / are buying* books only from the internet in a few years.
   c Who do you think *will win / are winning* the football match tonight?
3 What things would a learner need to know about new vocabulary items?
4 Write some concept checking questions for the grammatical pattern in bold:
   I'm going to go *to the shop. Is there anything you want?*
5 How can a teacher help to keep learners motivated?

B Reasons to test learners

1 Work in groups. Explain why the test may be taking place in the following testing situations.
   a A course director is expecting an intake of 100 students. They will all sit a test on the first morning of the course.
   b A teacher has a new class. In the second lesson she decides to give the class a short test.
   c A teacher has taught 50 hours of a 100-hour course. He decides to give the class a test.
   d A class is very near the end of their course. In the penultimate lesson they will have a test.

2 Work in small groups. Discuss the reasons teachers test learners. Are there disadvantages to testing learners?

C Ways of testing

1 Study the table and answer the questions. Which test types:
   a test individual language items?
   b test language items in combination?
   c test knowledge about language?
   d test language use?
   e can be marked objectively?
   f require subjective marking criteria?

Test types	Examples
Multiple-choice questions	*I'm .... to see Zoë tomorrow.* *a) gone b) go c) going d) went*
Gap-fill exercises	*She's very intelligent and I love .... accent.*
Sentence transformations	*The shop sold the last copy of the book yesterday.* *The last copy of the book ....*
Writing a composition	*You see the following job advert in a newspaper. Write a letter of application.*
Oral interviews	Learners are shown pictures and describe them orally.
Matching	Learners read a text and match pictures to the appropriate parts.
Sentence production	Learners write sentences about themselves using a given structure, such as *used to* + infinitive.

2 Which of the test types in activity C1 could be used to test the following areas?
  * receptive skills
  * productive skills
  * vocabulary and grammar

3 Work in groups. Decide what features make one learner's spoken language better than another's. For example:
  * One learner may use a wider range of vocabulary than another.

4 Now design some criteria by which you can assess performance in an oral test given to a group of learners. Use the table below to help you.

	A	B	C
Range of vocabulary and structures	A good range of vocabulary and structures	An adequate range of vocabulary and structures	An inadequate range of vocabulary and structures to communicate effectively
Fluency			
Accuracy (including pronunciation)			
Communication strategies			

D How not to test

Read the learners' complaints. Complete the sentences explaining the problem with the test design in each case.

> The instructions just said 'fill the gaps' – so I did and got nearly all of the questions wrong because I was only supposed to use one word. A lot of the students did the same as me.

a Instructions need …

> The course was all about listening and speaking and I really liked it – but at the end we had to do a writing test and I didn't do very well.

b The content of the test should …

> I got the test back from the teacher and I hadn't done very well. I was the worst in the class. The teacher just wrote 'You must work harder' at the bottom but I was working quite hard.

c Feedback should be …

E Analysing a test

1 Read the test on page 109. It comes at the end of a unit of an intermediate coursebook. What things do you think have been taught in the unit?

2 1 Do you think the writers of the test intended it to be done in an informal way, or more formally, more like an exam?

2 Would you ask the learners to do this test individually or in groups?

3 Do you like the type of questions that are asked?

4 Are there any sections that you would change?

Do you remember?

 1

Explain the difference in meaning (if any) between the following pairs of sentences.

a) • You mustn't eat that.
   • You shouldn't eat that.
b) • I must do some studying tonight.
   • I have to do some studying tonight.
c) • You mustn't write anything.
   • You don't have to write anything.
d) • I've got to stay in tonight.
   • I have to stay in tonight.
e) • She ought to be careful.
   • She should be careful.
f) • We must hurry.
   • We had to hurry.
g) • They couldn't sell alcohol.
   • They weren't allowed to sell alcohol.
h) • I didn't have to vote.
   • I wasn't allowed to vote.

 2

a) Match word partners in the box. Which word has no partner?

    strict   well-behaved   housework
    a rule   however   to obey
    liberal   therefore   homework
    badly-behaved   to punish
    to be alone   to disobey
    to be healthy   a law   to be lonely
    disadvantage   a punishment
    despite this   as a result
    to be unhealthy

b) Spend three minutes trying to memorise the words. Close your book and write them down – there are a total of twenty-one! Compare answers with a partner. Who remembered the most words?

 3

Which word in the list rhymes with the word in bold?

a) **can't**: want / aren't / ant
b) **allowed**: cloud / road / bored
c) **ought**: out / boat / bought
d) **law**: know / four / now
e) **should**: cold / food / stood
f) **although**: so / cough / now

 4

There is a word missing in _five_ of the following sentences. Find the mistakes and correct them.

a) She's always shouting her children.
b) The teacher told them for being late.
c) In the end, her mother let her go to the party.
d) I'm going to do shopping. Do you want anything?
e) I think it depends the situation.
f) I agree with you.
g) They missed the bus so they had walk home.

 5

Think of:

a) two things people usually do in the kitchen.
b) two things you might do this evening.
c) two things people often do when they're at school or university.
d) two things you don't like doing.

All your answers should include phrases with _do_.

 6

Join the following sentences using _although, however, therefore, also, for this reason,_ or _what is more_.

a) It was the middle of winter. The weather wasn't cold.
b) The train drivers have not had a pay rise this year. They're going on strike.
c) He has been ill recently. He has had a lot of personal problems.
d) There was a bomb in the city centre last night. Most of the shops are open as normal today.
e) There has been a serious accident. There are a lot of traffic jams.

7

Look back through Module 11 and write two more revision questions of your own to ask other students.

Cutting Edge (Intermediate) Cunningham and Moor

F Other ways of monitoring progress

Read about other ways of monitoring learners' progress and answer the questions. Then compare ideas with a partner.

1 In each case, who does the assessing, the learner or the teacher?
2 Are all the ideas practical?
3 Whose idea do you like best and why?
4 Whose idea do you like least and why?

a Shaun

Every lesson is an opportunity for teachers to assess how well individuals are progressing. If you monitor what learners say and do closely, you will know if they are making progress.

b Laura

I ask learners to keep a learning diary – they make a few notes after each lesson saying what they thought the aim of the lesson was, what they learned, how much they understood and whether they liked it. Every now and then I take the diaries in and see how the learners think they are doing.

c Kirsty

I give learners a list of what we've done in class and next to each thing they have three columns – 'confident', 'ok' and 'need practice'. They tick the appropriate column for each thing and give it back and I get some idea of how they think they are doing.

REFLECTION

1 Answer the questions.

a Is it a good idea to tell learners in advance that they will have a test?
b Do learners always have to do tests on their own?
c Should learners practise doing tests?
d What are some of the differences between 'teaching' and 'testing'?

2 Assuming that the test in section A was to measure your progress on the CELTA course, to what extent do you think that it was valid?

3 Design a short test that would be appropriate for your own teaching practice learners.

25 Teaching exam classes

A Warm-up

1 Work in pairs. Study the table for 90 seconds. It shows three popular exams and their approximate level according to the Common European Framework. Ask questions about these exams. Then answer your partner's questions.

Common European Framework	Cambridge ESOL	IELTS	TOEFL	
			Pen-and-paper test	Computer test
C2 Mastery	Proficiency (CPE)	7.5	633	267
		7.0	600+	250+
C1 Operational proficiency	Certificate of Advanced English (CAE)	6.0–6.5	540+	207+
B2 Vantage	First Certificate (FCE)	5.0–5.5	500+	170+
B1 Threshold	Preliminary English Test (PET)	4.0–4.5	350+	75+
A2 Waystage	Key English Test (KET)	3.0–3.5	250+	50–
		2.0–3.0		
A1 Breakthrough				

Learning Teaching Scrivener

2 Work in pairs. Write some more questions about exams. How can you find out the answers?

B Teaching exam classes

1 Complete the text with sentences a–e. There is one sentence that you do not need to use.

How to teach an FCE class

Be aware of issues like learner motivation and classroom morale. Learners in exam classes tend to be more goal-oriented than those in a general English class. (1) .... You can help to maintain motivation by gradually building up to FCE-level tasks and language. Don't test at FCE level too soon by announcing in week two: 'Right, class. Today we're going to try an FCE listening paper' – far better to try just one listening task at a time. Tackling small chunks of the exam paper in this way minimises the risk of demotivating individuals or even the whole class.

(2) .... Setting quizzes based on the exam specifications – e.g. How much time do you have for the Reading paper? – can inject some fun into an otherwise dull or routine procedure.

Students need to be familiar with the exam conditions and requirements. However, it is essential to get a good balance between exam-style tasks and general skills development. (3) .... Be aware that reading and grammar/vocabulary exercises can be usefully set for homework with class time being used to discuss, explain and compare answers.

Try to instil good study habits from the start. What your students do outside the exam classroom is just as vital in preparing for the exam. (4) .... Encourage learners to keep a vocabulary notebook, organised in a way that is meaningful to them. Encouraging learners to take a degree of responsibility for their own progress has an added bonus of taking the pressure off you.

(from web article on www.flo-joe.co.uk)

a
An FCE class needn't (and shouldn't) consist of a diet of endless exam practice.

b
It is also worth going through this sample paper yourself, as this will help you see the exam through your students' eyes.

c
However, motivation and high morale can be very fragile things.

d
Often, the most successful learners are those who keep good records of their learning.

e
Part of your role as a teacher is to demystify the exam requirements.

2 Work in pairs. Do the four sentences you inserted provide an adequate summary of the text?

3 Read the text again and answer the questions.

   1 What skill(s) did this exercise test?

   2 Inserting sentences into a text is a popular test type in some public examinations. Do you think it is a fair test?

C Exam question types

Work in groups. Read these rubrics taken from common exam question types and answer the questions.

1 What language knowledge, skills and sub-skills could they be used to test?

2 Would the question format be useful in a non-exam-focused course?

   a Key word transformations

> **Complete the second sentence so that it has a similar meaning to the first sentence, using the word given. Do not change the word given. You must use between two and five words, including the word given.**
>
> Example: Jane went to the meeting but it wasn't really necessary.
>
>   Jane ..... *needn't have gone* ..... to the meeting. (gone)

   b Picture discussion

> **Look at these two photographs [examiner shows two photographs, one of a tidy bedroom with a desk and one of a work space in a library]. Discuss with your partner in which of these two places you would prefer to study. What other environments are good for studying?**

   c Transactional writing

> **Here is part of an email you receive from a friend.**
>
> > College isn't going so well at the moment. I find it really hard to organise my time and last semester I failed two exams because I just didn't manage to revise for them.
>
> **Write a reply to your friend, giving some advice on how they could prepare for exams.**

D Exam materials

Work in groups. Choose an exam-based coursebook and answer the questions.

1 Does the book give an outline of the exam?

2 Choose one unit from the book. Does the material look interesting and motivating?

3 Read the texts in the unit you have chosen. Can you identify activities to do before the text, during the reading/listening, and after the text?

4 How much of the unit would be useful for most learners, regardless of whether they wish to do an exam? How much is useful only if you are preparing for the exam?

5 Would any of the material be appropriate for the classes you have taught?

REFLECTION

Write four sentences that are relevant to the teaching of exam classes. On a separate piece of paper write the stems of the sentences. Give your partner the stems to complete. Compare your answers.

Exam class students are usually highly motivated.

Exam class students are usually ...

26 Choosing and using teaching resources

A Warm-up

1 Imagine you are going off to teach English to adults in a remote part of the world. There are absolutely no teaching resources available and no electricity. Weight restrictions limit what you can take with you. Choose three items from this list that you would take.

- six copies of a student's reference grammar plus exercises
- a year's subscription to an English language weekly newspaper
- a set of Cuisenaire rods
- the collected works of William Shakespeare
- a dozen copies of a current coursebook
- a phonemic chart (see page 156)
- a selection of graded readers at different levels
- a battery-operated digital audio recorder, plus speakers
- four copies of an advanced learner's dictionary
- a teacher's resource book of classroom games and warmers
- an encyclopedia
- a guitar
- a set of 100 magazine pictures mounted on card

2 Compare your answers to activity A1 with a partner's. Agree on a definitive list of three items. Then join with another pair and do the same again.

B Coursebooks

1 Work in groups. Write 8–10 questions you would ask when choosing a coursebook. For example:

- Does it have a grammar reference section?
- Is the material culturally appropriate?

2 Work in groups. Use the questions you wrote in activity B1 to evaluate the coursebook that you are currently using in your teaching practice classes.

B Classroom teaching

3 Coursebooks are usually published along with a number of supplementary components. Match the components (1–9) of the coursebook *Reward* with the descriptions (a–i) from the publisher's catalogue.

Reward

Component	Description
1 Student's Book	a Detailed teaching notes include four photocopiable tests with a marking system
2 Teacher's Book	b 50 minutes of material in a combination of drama and mini-documentaries
3 Practice Book	c Additional exercises for further practice of grammar and vocabulary
4 Grammar and Vocabulary Workbook	d Contains over 40 photocopiable communicative lessons with full teacher's notes; ideal for learners who want some Business English integrated into their General English course
5 Diskette	e Provides a 70-hour core syllabus of forty lessons and eight Progress Check lessons
6 CD-ROM	f Provides additional teaching material, in photocopiable format, to practise the main language points of each lesson
7 Video	g Provides a variety of tests for teachers to customise to suit their learners' needs
8 Resource Pack	h Designed for class use or self-study, providing further practice in grammar, vocabulary, reading, writing, listening and sounds work
9 Business Resource Pack	i Wide variety of interactive activity types and practice material; each section is automatically marked and a running total of each individual student's score is kept

Macmillan *English Language Teaching Catalogue* 2005

4 Decide which of the components of *Reward* you would consider essential and which optional if you were adopting this course.

C Adapting and supplementing

1 Read the following activity. How could you adapt it for the following situations?

a teaching one-to-one
b teaching a distance class, online
c teaching a group of academic writing learners

face2face (*Pre-Intermediate*) Redston and Cunningham

2 Work in groups. Discuss how you could supplement the above activity with some authentic reading or listening material (for use in a General English class of adults). Think about the following questions:

1 What kind of material could you use?
2 What would it be about?
3 Where could you look for this material?
4 What purposes would you be using it for?

D Technology and aids

1 Work in groups. Look at the 'mind map' of things that you can do with an audio recorder-player in the classroom. Then design a similar mind map for one of the items below.

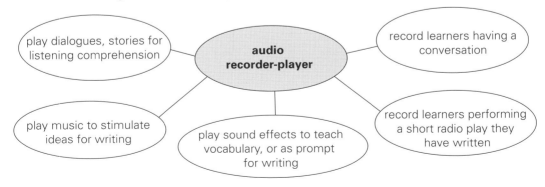

a DVD/video player
b video camera
c overhead projector/data projector

2 Work in groups. Read the list. Which of these language learning activities are now possible? By what technological means are they possible?

a Learners in different countries collaborate on a task in real time.
b Learners consult a database of real language, looking for examples of specific language items.
c Learners talk to a computer that speaks back.
d Learners' written compositions are automatically corrected.
e Learners watch English-language films with English subtitles.
f Learners read a text and get instant definitions of unfamiliar vocabulary.
g Learners get feedback on their pronunciation from a computer.
h Learners communicate with their teacher in out-of-class time, from wherever they happen to be.
i Learners take part in simulations using English.
j Learners get an instant print-out of the boardwork of a lesson.
k Learners assess the level of difficulty of an authentic text in advance of reading it.
l Learners' texts are automatically translated into English.
m Learners download audio lessons to listen to anywhere, at any time.

3 Read the extract from a report on the use of interactive whiteboards (IWBs) in schools. Decide which of these applications would be particularly useful in the *language* classroom.

Interactive whiteboards

An interactive whiteboard is a large, touch-sensitive board which is connected to a digital projector and a computer. The projector displays the image from the computer screen on the board. The computer can then be controlled by touching the board, either directly or with a special pen …

Ideal for:

- using web-based resources in whole-class teaching
- showing video clips to help explain concepts
- demonstrating a piece of software
- presenting learners' work to the rest of the class
- creating digital flipcharts
- manipulating text and practising handwriting
- saving notes written on the board for future use
- quick and seamless revision

(adapted from web article on www.becta.org)

E Teaching without technology

1 Imagine you are teaching in a place where resources are limited. How could you manage without coursebooks, audio or video equipment, or photocopying facilities? Suggest ways to do the following:

a grammar presentation
b grammar practice
c listening activities
d reading activities
e testing

2 Read the text and decide how the writer's view might be relevant to language learning.

I burnt most of my infant room material on Friday. I say that the more material there is for a child, the less pull there is on his own resources ... I burnt all the work of my youth. Dozens of cards made of three-ply and hand-printed and illustrated. Boxes of them. There will be only the following list in my infant room:

Chalk	Books
Blackboards	Charts
Paper	Paints
Pencils	Clay
Guitar	Piano

And when a child wants to read he can pick up a book with his own hands and struggle through it. The removal of effort and denying to the child of its right to *call on its own resources* ...
  (I was sad, though, seeing it all go up in smoke.)
  But teaching is so much simpler and clearer as a result. There's much more time for conversation ... communication. (You should have heard the roaring in the chimney!)

Teacher Sylvia Ashton-Warner

REFLECTION

Work in groups. Read these teachers' statements. To what extent do you agree with them?

a 'I structure my classes around the coursebook, but there may be whole lessons where we don't even open it.'

b 'A lot of the boring stuff associated with language learning can now be done by the learners working on their own, using computers, for example. This frees up the classroom for the really interesting stuff.'

c 'I could teach anywhere, so long as I had a blackboard.'

d 'Nowadays learners expect schools to have state-of-the-art resources and they also expect that teachers will use them. Not to do so might be considered unprofessional.'

27 Introduction to language analysis

A Warm-up

Match the terms (1–10) with their definitions (a–j).

Terms used to talk about language	Definitions
1 vocabulary	a the rules that govern the way words are combined and sequenced in order to form sentences
2 grammar	b the purpose for which a language item is used
3 structure	c the place in the world where an instance of language occurs, or the words surrounding it in a text
4 concept	d the way that sounds are produced when speaking a language
5 function	e the area of language learning that is concerned with word knowledge
6 style	f a continuous piece of speech or writing, having a communicative purpose and a distinctive organisation
7 pronunciation	g a grammar pattern that generates examples, such as the present perfect
8 context	h the way that words or structures are written or pronounced
9 text	i variation in a person's use of language due to situational factors, such as context and degree of familiarity
10 form	j the basic meaning of a word or structure, independent of context

B Multiple perspectives

1 When analysing language, any piece of 'real-life' language can be looked at from different points of view. Read this authentic text and decide which term in the warm-up activity defines each feature.

> Passengers are reminded that baggage must not be left unattended. Baggage found unattended will be removed and may be destroyed.

- impersonal, formal; written in order to be read aloud = 6 style
- warning
- stress on main information words (*PASSengers, reMINDed, BAGGage, unatTENDed…*); intonation falls at the end of each sentence
- use of modal verbs (*must, will, may*) and passive voice (*are reminded, be removed, be destroyed*)
- words associated with travel (*passengers, baggage*); verbs associated with security practices (*removed, destroyed*)
- an airport

2 Read the following text and identify:

a the text type
b the context in which it is typically found
c its function
d its style
e any sets of words that relate to the topic of the text
f any distinctive features of its grammar

For the perfect cup

Use one teabag per person and add freshly drawn boiling water.
Leave standing for 3–5 minutes before stirring gently.
Can be served with or without milk and sugar.

Vocabulary is dealt with in Unit 38.
Text organisation is dealt with in Unit 39.

C Parts of speech

In English there are at least eight parts of speech. These are:

* nouns, e.g. *passengers, baggage, tea, minutes*
* pronouns, i.e. words that take the place of nouns, such as *it, they*
* verbs, e.g. *are, be, use, stirring, destroyed*
* adjectives, e.g. *perfect, unattended*
* adverbs, e.g. *freshly, gently*
* prepositions, e.g. *for, with, without*
* determiners, e.g. the definite article *the*, the indefinite article *a/an*, and words like *one, some, this*, which go in front of nouns
* conjunctions, i.e. words that join parts of sentences, such as *and, or, that*

Many common words can function as different parts of speech, depending on their context. Thus, *that* is a conjunction in *Passengers are reminded <u>that</u> baggage must not be left unattended*. But it is a determiner in a sentence like *Whose is <u>that</u> baggage?* And it is a pronoun in the sentence *Whose is <u>that</u>?*

Work in pairs. Identify the part of speech of each word in the following film titles. Note that if a pair of words is contracted, for example in the case of *it's*, the pair should be analysed as two separate words: *it + is*.

a *It's A Wonderful Life*
b *Gentlemen Prefer Blondes*
c *It Happened One Night*
d *A Funny Thing Happened On The Way To The Forum*
e *The Postman Always Rings Twice*
f *I Married A Monster From Outer Space*
g *And God Created Woman*
h *Stop! Or My Mom Will Shoot*

121

D Sentence elements

Words group together to form meaningful units called *phrases*. Each phrase forms an element that fulfils a specific *function* in the sentence. For example:

Subject (identifies the actor or agent)	Verb (expresses a process or state)	Adverbial (gives circumstantial information, such as time, place or manner)
A funny thing	*happened*	*on the way to the forum*

Subject	Verb	Object (identifies the person or thing affected)
I	*married*	*a monster from outer space*
Gentlemen	*prefer*	*blondes*

Subject	Verb	Complement (gives additional information about the subject)
It	*is*	*a wonderful life*

Work in pairs. Divide these film titles into their component phrases and assign a function to each phrase. Note that sometimes a phrase can consist of only one word.

a *It Happened One Night*
b *Mr Smith Goes To Washington*
c *Lady Sings The Blues*
d *The Empire Strikes Back*
e *I Was A Teenage Werewolf*
f *The Russians Are Coming*
g *Who Framed Roger Rabbit?*
h *Meet Me In St Louis*
i *I Never Promised You A Rose Garden*

E Contrastive analysis

1 Read the sentences with their translations and answer the questions.

1 Are the elements in the sentence (e.g. subject, verb, object) in the same order as in English or a different one?

2 Are the elements in a phrase (e.g. article, adjective, noun) in the same order as in English or a different one?

3 Are there elements that occur in English but not in the other language – and vice versa?

a **Turkish**

Ingliz   kitapları   odamda
English   books-the   room-my-in
(The English books are in my room)

Biz   yine   eski   hayatımıza   döndük
we   again   old   life-our-to   returned
(We returned to our old life again)

b **Arabic**

buyūtu   al-rajuli   al-ghanīyi   ɛalā   nahrin
houses   the man   the rich   on   river
(The rich man's houses are on a river)

hādhā   khitābun   baɛathathu   sayyidatun   shahīratun
this   letter   sent-it   lady   famous
(This is a letter which a famous lady sent)

c **Japanese**

ringo- o   tabeta
apple-[OBJECT marker]   ate
(He ate an apple)

zoo-wa   hana-ga   nagai
elephant-[TOPIC marker]   nose-[SUBJECT marker]   long
(Elephants have long noses)

watashi-wa   mise-he   ikimasu.
I-[TOPIC marker]   store-to   go
(I go to the store)

Hanoko-ga   Taro-ni kompyūtā-o   ageta
Hanoko-[SUBJECT marker] Taro-to computer-[OBJECT marker] gave
(Hanoko gave Taro a computer)

2 Work in pairs. Discuss what errors speakers of each of the languages in activity E3 might make in English.

REFLECTION

Look at the contents page of a coursebook that you are using (or that you have used). Find the grammar items that constitute the syllabus (or part of it). Choose one item that you are *not* familiar with. What guidance does the book provide that might help you analyse this item? For example, is there a grammar reference section at the back? Do you think the book gives a sufficiently detailed description? Is it easy to follow? (You may have to consult the Teacher's Book, too.)

28 Tense and aspect

A Warm-up

Work in pairs. Do the quiz.

1 How many tenses are there in English?
   a 2   b 3   c 6   d 24

2 In the question *Where do you live?* what is *do?*
   a an infinitive   b a participle   c an auxiliary verb   d a modal verb

3 In the question *Where have you been?* what is *been?*
   a an infinitive   b a participle   c an auxiliary verb   d a modal verb

4 Which is the odd one out in this group? Why?
   a went   b done   c came   d began

5 Which of the following time expressions is unlikely with this sentence, and why? *She's seeing Peter.*
   a now   b always   c tomorrow   d yesterday

6 Which of the following time expressions is unlikely with this sentence, and why?
   I've been to Guatemala.
   a never   b last year   c once   d many times

B Tense review

1   Read this extract from a magazine article and:
   a   name the verb form in each of the underlined verb phrases.
   b   find one more example of each form in the text.

Jo Thornley, 57, <u>runs</u> her own plumbing business from Ilkley, West Yorkshire. She's married with two grown-up children.

'When I <u>told</u> my friends and family I <u>was training</u> as a plumber, some of them were horrified. They didn't think it was a suitable job for a woman and my mother-in-law said to me, "Surely you don't want to drive around in a van with your name on it?" But I knew it was what I wanted.

At 42, I was a French teacher, but I'<u>d become</u> very unhappy with what was happening in schools. I'd always liked the idea of being a plumber, because it's such a useful job – someone's got a leak or their heating <u>isn't working</u>, and you can sort it out for them. I've got as much work as I want and I really enjoy it.

I'm aware that I'm not as strong as the men, especially now I'm getting older, so I'<u>ve taken</u> on an apprentice. That's worked really well: he's got the strength and I've got the knowledge.

I'm very proud of what I've achieved, and there's a real sense of satisfaction in having learned something completely new. To anyone thinking of making a change like I did, I'd say, "Just go for it!"'

(from article in *Woman's Weekly*)

2 Complete the table using examples from the text in activity B 1.

Tense	Aspect	Examples
present	(no aspect = simple)	
	continuous	
	perfect	
past	(no aspect = simple)	
	continuous	
	perfect	

C Basic concepts

One way to understand the basic concepts of the different verb forms is to contrast them.

1 Work in pairs. What is the difference in meaning between these pairs of sentences?

1 a Jo Thornley runs her own plumbing business.
   b Jo Thornley ran her own plumbing business.
2 a I was a French teacher.
   b I am a French teacher.
3 a Jo Thornley runs her own plumbing business.
   b Jo Thornley is running her own plumbing business.
4 a Their heating isn't working.
   b Their heating doesn't work.
5 a I'm very proud of what I achieve.
   b I'm very proud of what I've achieved.
6 a I've taken on an apprentice.
   b I took on an apprentice.
7 a I trained as a plumber.
   b I was training as a plumber.
8 a I'd become very unhappy.
   b I became very unhappy.

2 Match the verb forms (1–6) with their main concepts (a–f):

Verb form	Concept
1 present simple	a past event with present relevance
2 past simple	b activity or process, in progress in the past
3 present continuous	c past state, event or habit
4 past continuous	d present state, event or habit
5 present perfect	e past event that happened prior to another past event
6 past perfect	f activity or process, in progress in the present

D Learner problems

Study these learner errors. How would you explain to the learners the correct rule in each case?

a I am not enjoy this film. Let's leave.
b What do you eating now?
c Yesterday I and my friend go to the swimming pool.
d I studied for the exam but I didn't passed.
e What have you done last holidays?
f I met my friend when I walked in the park.
g When we arrived the film already started.

E Materials

Study these teaching materials.

a What verb form does each one target?
b Is the focus on form or meaning – or both?
c In the case of meaning, what exact meaning is targeted?

2.2 *This time you have to read some sentences and correct them. The English is correct but the information is wrong. Write two correct sentences each time.*

Example: The sun goes round the earth. The sun doesn't go round the earth.
The earth goes round the sun.

1   The sun rises in the west. ....
....

2   Mice catch cats. ....
....

3   Carpenters make things from metal. ....
....

4   The River Amazon flows into the Pacific Ocean. ....
....

English Grammar in Use Murphy

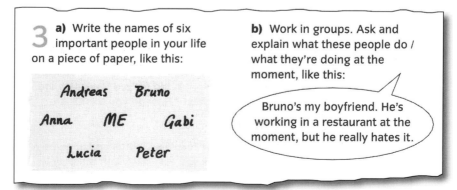

Cutting Edge (Intermediate) Cunningham and Moor

> **1 Talk to other students and complete this chart. What questions
> will you ask each student?**
>
> | Who has done these things for | the shortest / longest time? | |
> |---|---|---|
> | | (name/time) | (name/time) |
> | Been in this town/country
Known their best friend/partner
Had their own room/house
Been able to drive
Played their favourite sport | | |

The Intermediate Choice Mohamed and Acklam

F Classroom application

Work in groups. Your trainer will assign your group one of the grammar items (a–f). Devise a way of presenting this item.

a present simple with adverbs of frequency (such as *always, often, sometimes, never*)
b present continuous for activities in progress at the time of speaking
c present continuous for future arrangements
d present perfect for recent events, using *just*
e present perfect for situations continuing to the present, using *for/since*
f present perfect passive for changes that have present results (for example: *The school has been decorated.*)

Your presentation should include:

• a situation which illustrates the meaning of the item
• at least three or four examples of the item
• some kind of check of understanding, such as concept questions or timelines.

Identify any visual aids that would facilitate your presentation.

Be prepared to demonstrate your presentation idea to the rest of the class.

REFLECTION

1 Read these sentence beginnings. In each case, think of a way of continuing each sentence so that its meaning is clear.

The bus leaves …
The bus is leaving …
The bus has left …

2 Check that you can now answer the questions in the quiz at the beginning of this unit correctly.

29 Meaning, form and use: the past

A Warm-up

Work in groups of three. Two of you will have a conversation and one will observe and take notes.
Speakers: Choose one of the following and take turns to tell each other about it.
Note-taker: Your trainer will give you details of what to listen for.

- a strange, frightening, or funny encounter with an animal
- the last wedding you went to
- a 'small world' experience you once had
- a time when you lost something important
- a time when you saw a famous person by chance
- the first time you took a flight on your own

B Past verb forms

1 Work in pairs. Match the rules (1–6) with the examples (a–f).

Rules about the formation of the past simple	Examples
1 To form the past simple of regular verbs, add -(e)d to the base form of the verb (i.e. the infinitive without to).	a /d/ as in *rained*; /t/ as in *liked*; and /ɪd/ as in *started*.
2 Verbs that end in consonant + -y, change the -y to -i; and verbs that end in a single vowel + a single consonant, double the consonant.	b *Did it rain? Why didn't they like it?*
3 The -(e)d ending is pronounced in three different ways.	c *rained, liked, started, finished*, etc.
4 There are many irregular verbs, which have to be learned as individual items.	d *carry* → *carried*; *stop* → *stopped*
5 Both regular and irregular verbs form their negatives with *did not* (*didn't*) + the base form.	e *It didn't rain. They didn't like it.*
6 Questions are formed by inverting the subject and the auxiliary verb *did*, + the base form.	f *went, made, came, cut, wrote*, etc.

2 Decide which of the rules refers specifically to the spoken form, and which refers specifically to the written form.

3 Complete the table, adding the missing rules or providing examples.

Rules about the formation of the past continuous	Examples
1 The past continuous is formed with *was* or *were* + *-ing* (the present participle).	
2	*It wasn't raining. They weren't watching.*
3	*Was it raining? What were they doing?*
4 Negative questions are formed by adding *not* ('nt) to the auxiliary verb.	

4 Write the rules for these examples of how the past perfect is formed.

Rules about the formation of the past perfect	Examples
1	*It had rained. Someone had taken it. The train had left.*
2	*It hadn't rained. The train hadn't left.*
3	*Had it rained? Why hadn't the train left?*

The different tenses of the verb are dealt with in Unit 28.

C Focus on meaning

1 Complete the timelines for each of the sentences below.

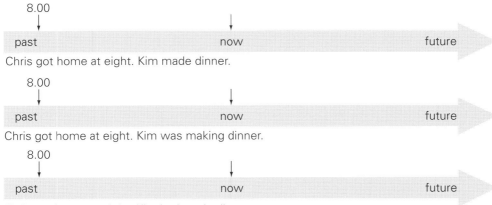

8.00

past   now   future

Chris got home at eight. Kim made dinner.

8.00

past   now   future

Chris got home at eight. Kim was making dinner.

8.00

past   now   future

Chris got home at eight. Kim had made dinner.

2 Formulate a general rule about the meaning of each of these past tense forms.

past simple: ....

past continuous: ....

past perfect: ....

D Focus on use

Read this extract from the beginning of a short story and identify:

a one example of each of the past tense forms that you have been studying in this session.
b which tense form the writer uses to tell the main events of the narrative.
c which tense form he uses to describe ongoing background activities.
d which tense form he uses to fill in details retrospectively.

> My wife and I were driving south on Highway 54 from Alamogordo to El Paso. We'd spent the afternoon at White Sands and my brain was still scorched from the glare. […] Jessica was driving. It was early evening. We were about sixty miles south of Alamogordo and the light was fading. A freight train was running parallel to the road, also heading south.
>
> 'Hitch-hiker!' I said, pointing. 'Shall we pick him up?'
>
> 'Shall we?' My wife was slowing down. We could see him more clearly now, a black guy in his late twenties. […] We slowed to a crawl and took a good look at him. He looked fine. I lowered my window, the passenger window. He had a nice smile.
>
> 'Where ya going?' he said.
>
> 'El Paso,' I said.

White Sands Geoff Dyer

E Learners' problems

1 Read these examples of learner language. Identify and correct any errors in the use of past tense forms.

a It is unbelievable how Gandhi fighted against Britain only with his hope of peace.
b When I was a child I was going to the beach every summer.
c After I heared the news I don't stopped crying.
d When I opened the door, I saw a strange man. He weared a military dress.
e As soon as we arrived we realised that Maria's baggage didn't arrive.
f Last weekend I felt very bad so I spended all day on the bed.
g When we were finishing the desserts the doorbell rangs.
h I thought that he would be in the kitchen eating something, but he didn't be there.
i The bus drivers go on strike. That's why we decided to go by train.
j It was late. I had been waiting half an hour at the bus stop, but the bus still didn't have arrived.

2 Work in pairs. Answer the questions.

• Which of the examples in activity E1 show the correct choice of tense, but are not well formed?
• Which examples in activity E1 show the wrong choice of tense, even though they are well formed?
• Which errors in activity E1 display a mixture of both?

3 Work in groups. Draw up a list of problems learners have with past tense forms.

F Classroom application

1 Work in groups. Your trainer will assign your group one of the following structures. Decide how you could present the structure so that its meaning, form and use are clear.

  a the past continuous for actions that are interrupted, e.g. *When I was writing my assignment, my computer crashed.*

  b the past of the verb *to be* (i.e. *was, were*)

  c reported speech statements, as in *Elsie told him there wasn't anybody home.*

  d past simple questions, e.g. *Where did you stay?*

  e past perfect with verbs of cognition, as in *I realised I had left my wallet at home.*

2 Compare your presentations with another group.

> **REFLECTION**
>
> Find a unit in a coursebook you are using or have used that deals with the past simple, the past continuous or the past perfect. Identify activities that deal with, respectively, the meaning, the form, *and* the use of the structure.

30 Expressing future meaning

A Warm-up

1 Complete this coursebook activity.

> Complete the following sentences in any way that is true for you.
>
> a Once this lesson has finished …
> b The moment I get home today …
> c When I have enough money …
> d As soon as I have some free time …
> e When I'm next on holiday …
> f This time next year …
> g In five years' time …
> h By the time I retire …
>
> Compare your sentences with a partner's.

Inside Out (Upper-Intermediate) Kay and Jones

2 Work in groups. Read the sentences you have all written and answer the questions.

1 What grammar structures can you identify?
2 Did you all use the same structures to finish the sentences?
3 If your answer to 2 was 'no', how did the choice of structure affect the meaning?

B Future forms

1 Study this grammar explanation from the coursebook used in A1 and identify the grammar structures you used in the warm-up activity.

Language reference: future forms

Will ('ll), (be) going to, present continuous

These are the three most common forms for talking about the future.

1 *Will ('ll)* – predictions/decisions reacting to circumstances such as offers, promises and requests.
It'll be worth a fortune in a few years' time.
I'll give you my photograph now if you like.

2 *(be) going to* – intentions/predictions based on present evidence.
I'm going to concentrate on my musical career.
Look at those clouds. It's going to pour down.

3 The present continuous – plans/arrangements
I'm moving to London next month.

Present simple

You can use this form to talk about fixed future events: timetables, routines, schedules.
My A-levels start next week.
The plane leaves at 15:40.

Might & may

If you want to speculate about a future possibility you can use *might* or *may*.
We might have to get a part-time job.

132

2 Decide whether the explanations match your own use of these structures.

3 Work in pairs. Discuss in what order and at what levels you would expect these structures to be first introduced. Consider factors such as:

  * usefulness
  * frequency
  * difficulty – of form and of concept

C Learner problems

1 Read these sentences that learners wrote in response to the warm-up activity above. Identify and correct the errors they have made in using the different future forms.

  a The moment I get home today I going to play a computer game. Then to eat a sandwich.
  b Once this lesson has finished I meet my friend because we go to the cinema. After maybe we take a coffee in any café.
  c Once this lesson has finished I'll go to my house. I'll read the newspaper and prepare a nice dinner. I won't watch TV.
  d When I have enough money … I never will have enough money! But if I will, I will visit many countries.
  e When I'm next on holiday I am spending a good time with my family.
  f This time next year I will study for my final examination. I think my life won't be much different.
  g In five years' time may be I am going to have a better job. I'll like to start my own business.
  h By the time I retire I hope I will save enough money for buy a nice house by Black Sea.

2 Work in pairs. Discuss how you would explain the corrections to the learners.

3 Read the following sentences. Decide what problems of pronunciation you would expect learners to have in producing them.

  a The children won't go to bed.
  b What'll you do if it rains?
  c Where shall we go?

> **Future continuous**
>
> You use this tense to talk about something happening around a certain time in the future.
> *In five years' time I'll be staying in posh hotels.*
> *This time next week I'll be trekking in Nepal.*
>
> **Future perfect**
>
> You use the future perfect to talk about something completed by a certain time in the future.
> *By this time next year, we'll have had a record in the charts.*
> *The builder will have finished the kitchen walls by the end of the week.*
>
> **Verb structures after *if, when, as soon as* …**
>
> When it is clear from the main clause that the sentence is about the future you don't use a future form in the subordinate clause.
> *When I leave school, I'm going to concentrate on my musical career.* (NOT ~~When I will leave school~~, …)
> *It'll be a miracle if she's passed the exam.*
> (NOT … ~~if she will have passed the exam~~.)
>
> Other conjunctions which introduce subordinate clauses: *after, as soon as, before, once, the moment, the minute, unless, until.*

Inside Out (Upper-Intermediate) Kay and Jones

D Grammar presentation (1)

1 Study the coursebook presentation and identify:

   a the structure that is the focus of the presentation
   b the particular concept that is being targeted
   c the means by which the concept is conveyed
   d ways that the learners' understanding of both the form and the meaning is checked

Language focus 2
Predictions: *will* and *won't*

Matt, from London, is visiting the capital city of your country in August. What do you say to him?

a It'll be hot.
b You'll have a wonderful time.
c There'll be lots of tourists.
d You won't see the city at its best.
e It won't be very crowded.
f You'll have to take warm clothes with you.
g There'll be lots of insects.
h You won't be able to find a hotel.

Grammar

1 Tick (✓) the correct answer. Sentences a–h above describe:
   a things you plan to do.
   b things you expect to happen.
   c things you want to happen.

2 a What does *'ll* mean in *It'll be hot*?
   b What does *won't* mean in *You won't see the city at its best*?
   c Change this sentence into a question.
   There'll be lots of tourists.

Cutting Edge (Pre-Intermediate) Cunningham and Moor

2 Work in pairs. Think of ways you could follow up this presentation with a practice activity.

E Grammar presentation (2)

1 Study this coursebook presentation in which two structures are contrasted, and identify:

   a the structures that are being contrasted
   b the two concepts that are being contrasted
   c the means by which the contrast is conveyed

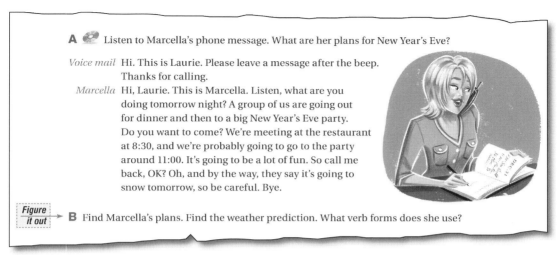

A 🎧 Listen to Marcella's phone message. What are her plans for New Year's Eve?

Voice mail Hi. This is Laurie. Please leave a message after the beep. Thanks for calling.

Marcella Hi, Laurie. This is Marcella. Listen, what are you doing tomorrow night? A group of us are going out for dinner and then to a big New Year's Eve party. Do you want to come? We're meeting at the restaurant at 8:30, and we're probably going to go to the party around 11:00. It's going to be a lot of fun. So call me back, OK? Oh, and by the way, they say it's going to snow tomorrow, so be careful. Bye.

Figure it out **B** Find Marcella's plans. Find the weather prediction. What verb forms does she use?

Touchstone 2 McCarthy, McCarten and Sandiford

2 Work in pairs. Devise a practice activity that requires students to discriminate between the two forms presented in activity E1.

F Classroom application

Work in groups. Devise a short presentation contrasting *will* (for making decisions) and *going to* (for talking about plans). Your presentation should include:

* a situation that contextualises the two structures, e.g. a dialogue or a monologue
* a task that requires the learners to focus on the contrast
* a way of checking learners' understanding of the contrast

Be prepared to demonstrate your presentation.

REFLECTION

Do the quiz.

1 Does English have a future tense?
2 What are the three most common ways of expressing future meaning in English?
3 Which two structures can be used to make predictions?
4 Which structure is typically used to talk about timetables and schedules in the future?
5 Which of the following factors determine the choice of future form? (You can choose more than one.)

a the speaker's purpose, e.g. making a prediction, talking about arrangements, etc.
b the speaker's assessment of the certainty of the future situation
c the extent that the future situation is seen to be connected to the present
d the speaker's assessment of how soon the future situation is
e the degree of informality

31 Modality

A Warm-up

Study these example sentences and answer the questions.

> a They have been swimming.
> b They must have been swimming.
> c She may swim.

1 How many verbs are there in each sentence?
2 Which verb carries the main meaning (i.e. which is the *lexical verb*) in each sentence?
3 In sentence a, what is the purpose of the other verb(s)?
4 Which sentence (a or b) states a fact and which expresses the speaker's belief about, or attitude to, the fact?
5 In sentence b, which verb is the 'attitude' verb (i.e. the *modal verb*)?
6 In what context(s) would sentence b be more appropriate than sentence a?
7 What is the modal verb in sentence c?
8 What are the two different meanings of sentence c?

Now write two or three questions about *modal verbs* that you would like answered.

B Modal verbs in context

Modal verbs are auxiliary verbs (or 'helping verbs') that convey the speaker's attitude to the events being talked about, and specifically such meanings as the *necessity*, *probability* or *desirability* of the event.

1 Read the text and identify the modal verbs. There are eight different ones; some are repeated.

CABIN CREW POSITIONS

We are currently recruiting **cabin crew for London Gatwick and Leeds-Bradford airports** on a permanent basis. Applicants will be at least 18 years old, must hold a 10-year British or European passport, and should be fluent in English and at least one other European language. We are also recruiting cabin crew who can speak fluent Arabic for our long haul operation.

We are looking for tactful, and resourceful people who are able to interact comfortably with strangers and remain calm under duress. Please note that the job can be physically demanding. A high standard of physical fitness is essential. What's more, cabin crew have to be prepared to work on any day of the year, at any time of the day.

Previous experience is not required. Successful applicants must attend and pass a four-week training course before they may graduate as flight attendants.

If you meet all our requirements and would like to be considered for a position as a flight attendant, please request an application form.

2 Read the text again and answer the questions.
  1 Two of the modal verbs in the text are followed by *to* + infinitive: which are they?
  2 Why do you think the (six) others are called 'pure' modals? Think of any other pure modals that are not in the text. (There are at least three more.)
  3 Decide which modals in the text express:
   * necessity
   * probability
   * ability
   * desirability
   * permission
  4 'Previous experience is not required.' Which of these sentences expresses the same idea?
   i You don't have to have previous experience.
   ii You mustn't have previous experience.

Modal verbs: form

1 Study these rules that govern the 'pure' modals. Match the rules with the examples.

Rule	Examples
1 The negative is formed by adding *not* (contracted to *n't*).	a *Shall we dance?* *What would I do without you?*
2 There is no *-s* in the third person singular.	b *I could have danced all night.* *You must have been a beautiful baby.*
3 There is no *do/does* in the question.	c *We can work it out.* *I'll follow the sun.*
4 They are followed by the infinitive without *to*.	d *Every Jack should have a Jill.* *It might as well be spring.*
5 They can be used with *have* + past participle to talk about the past.	e *I can't take my eyes off you.* *We mustn't say goodbye.*

2 As well as the 'pure' modals, there are equivalent phrase-like modal structures that use verbs like *have* or *going*, or adjectives like *able* or *allowed*. These *modal phrases* do not follow the rules in the table above, but they do have modal meaning.
Match the pure modals (1–6) with their modal phrase equivalents (a–f).

Modal verbs	Modal phrases
1 *You must do it.*	a *You're able to do it.*
2 *You will do it.*	b *You're not allowed to do it.*
3 *You can do it.*	c *You have to do it.*
4 *You should do it.*	d *You don't have to do it.*
5 *You may not do it.*	e *You're going to do it.*
6 *You needn't do it.*	f *You'd better do it.*

Note that these are not always exact equivalents: *you must do it* and *you have to do it*, for example, are not always interchangeable. And, as we saw above, the negative of *must* (*mustn't*) is very different from the negative of *have to* (*don't have to*).

D Modal verbs: meaning and use

All the pure modal verbs express *possibility/probability* (including future *predictability*). But they can express other meanings as well. These other meanings include: *ability*, *willingness* (also called *volition*), *necessity* (including *obligation*), *prohibition*, *permission* and *desirability*. Note that these meanings are typically concerned with the way that people interact and interrelate, hence they are sometimes called *interpersonal* meanings.

1 Study the pairs of sentences (a–f). Identify the sentence in each pair that expresses possibility/probability. Then identify the interpersonal meaning expressed by the same modal verb in the other sentence.

For example:
 i You **should** really wear a tie: it's a formal reception.
 ii It **should** be a good party: why don't you come?

Sentence ii) contains a modal verb that expresses possibility/probability; the interpersonal meaning expressed by the same modal verb in sentence i) is obligation.

   a   i 'What's the weather like?' 'They say it **may** rain.'
       ii **May** I take one of these brochures?
   b   i Excuse me, you **can't** smoke in here.
       ii She **can't** be engaged: she's not wearing a ring.
   c   i Some dogs **will** bite if you provoke them.
       ii **Will** you please be quiet!
   d   i I **must** phone Kate: it's her birthday.
       ii 'Who broke the window?' 'It **must** have been the children.'
   e   i When I was your age I **could** walk on my hands.
       ii Take a pullover. It **could** get cold.
   f   i **Wouldn't** it be nice if your father was here?
       ii The car **wouldn't** start so we had to push it.

2 Write sentences including a modal verb or modal phrase to express these functions.

   a asking permission
      May I sit down? Can we leave our bags here?
   b giving advice
   c asking someone to do something
   d offering to do something
   e promising
   f stating an intention
   g inviting

3 Work in groups of three. Identify real-life situations where the functions in D2 are likely to occur.
For example:

   a asking permission: in a museum, e.g. asking permission to take photographs

Language functions are dealt with in Unit 33.

E Classroom application

1 Study these examples of coursebook materials that deal with modality. In each case:

a identify the modal verb (or verbs) that the exercise focuses on

b identify the particular meaning(s), e.g. probability, ability, permission, volition, etc., that the exercise focuses on

c decide if the exercise is aimed at first-time presentation, or if it is a practice exercise.

---

speaking it's your turn!

1 You're going to sell three of your things (your book, your pen, etc.). Choose three things and decide a price for each one.

examples   my jacket – €80   my pencil – 30 cents

2 Try to sell your things to a partner. They should try to get a discount.

example   A   How much is your jacket?
        B   It's €80.
        A   €80! That's expensive. I'll give you €50.
        B   No, but you can have it for €70.
        A   No thanks, I'll leave it. / OK, I'll take it.

3 Move around the class. Try to buy things at a discount.

4 Tell the class what you bought. Who got the best price?

Natural English (Pre-Intermediate) Gairns and Redman

2 Mistakes

could/needn't/should(n't) have done

1 Here is the end of a story. Choose the structures that you think fit the meaning best.

… Of course, as soon as I went in the room, I realised that I *needn't/shouldn't* have spent all that time dressing up in a dinner jacket. I *could/should* have just worn jeans, like everyone else.

Now look at these other two stories.
How do you think they end?

… and there was a police truck towing away our car. It was our own fault, of course. We …

… It was only when I finally staggered up to the ninth floor that I realised that 'Aufzug' means 'lift'. So it turned out that I …

2 Think of a time when something similar happened to you, and write a sentence about it using one of the structures in the box.

Tell another student what happened.
Include your sentence in what you say.

could have	should have
needn't have	shouldn't have

Language in Use (Upper-Intermediate) Doff and Jones

C Language awareness

At what age can I ...?

5 You have to go to school!
You have to pay to go on trains, buses, etc.
You can drink alcohol in private – for example at home.

10 You can be convicted of a criminal offence.

12 You can buy a pet.

13 You can get a part-time job, but you can't work for more than two hours on a school day or on a Sunday.

14 You can go into a pub but you can't buy or drink alcohol there.

16 You can leave school.
You can marry but you must have your parents' consent.
A boy can join the armed forces with his parents' consent.
You can buy cigarettes and tobacco.
You can have beer, cider, or wine with a meal in a restaurant.

17 You can have a licence to drive most vehicles.
You can go to prison.

18 You reach the 'age of majority' – you are an adult in the eyes of the law.
You can vote in elections.
You can open a bank account.
You can buy alcohol in a pub.

21 You can become a Member of Parliament.

The Guardian / Children's Legal Centre

Reading
Finding specific information

1 How old do you have to be to do these things in your country?

- [ ] go to school
- [ ] drink alcohol
- [ ] leave school
- [ ] marry
- [ ] drive
- [ ] vote
- [ ] pay on public transport
- [ ] buy cigarettes
- [ ] work for money

2 ☀ **Against the clock!** In pairs, read the text in five minutes. Find out when you can do the things in ex.1 in England and Wales.

3 Which age restrictions are unfair? Why? Compare in pairs.

Clockwise (Intermediate) Forsyth

2 Your trainer will assign you one of the following modal structures. Write a short dialogue (six to eight lines) to contextualise it:

a *should/shouldn't* (advice)

b *have to/don't have to* (obligation)

c *could've, might've, can't have* (deduction about the past)

3 Work in groups. Discuss how you would present and exploit your dialogue. Be prepared to demonstrate it to the class.

REFLECTION

1 Complete the coursebook exercise below.

Find and correct the grammar mistake in each of the following sentences.

a Do you can help me a minute?

b What time have you to start work?

c I must to go now. Bye-bye.

d We no allowed to wear jeans at school.

e We no can do what we want.

f I mustn't do the laundry because my mother does it for me.

g You can't smoking in here. It's against the rules.

h My mother have to work very hard six days a week.

New Headway (Intermediate) Soars and Soars

2 Work in pairs. Identify the rule that is being broken in each of the sentences in the exercise in Reflection 1.

3 Work in groups. Review the questions you wrote in the warm-up activity. Identify any points you are still unsure about. Discuss possible answers to your questions. If necessary, ask your trainer to help.

140

32 Conditionals and hypothetical meaning

A Warm-up

1 Work in pairs. Match the beginnings (1–10) with the endings (a–j) of these song lines. (And do you know who sang them?)

1 If I was your girlfriend …	a … the love I would've shown.
2 If you ever leave me …	b … what a wonderful world this would be.
3 Where would you be …	c … I don't want to be right.
4 If you don't know me by now …	d … don't mention my name.
5 If every day could be just like Christmas …	e … will you take me with you?
6 If I had only known, …	f … you will never, never, never know me.
7 If loving you is wrong …	g … would you let me wash your hair?
8 If I could turn back time, if I could find a way …	h … if he walked into my life today?
9 If you talk in your sleep …	i … I'd take back those words that have hurt you.
10 Would I make the same mistakes …	j … if you weren't here with me?

2 Decide which of the song lines express unreal (i.e. hypothetical) situations.

B Conditional sentences

1 Read this description from a grammar reference book and answer the questions.

Conditional sentences are usually divided into three basic types referred to as Type 1, Type 2 and Type 3. Each has its own variations, but the elements are as follows:

> **Type 1**: *What will you do if you lose your job?*
> Asking/talking about something that is quite possible:
> **'if' + present + 'will'**
> *If I **lose** my job I **will go** abroad.*
>
> **Type 2**: *What would you do if you lost your job?*
> Asking/talking about imagined situations/consequences now:
> **'if' + past + 'would'**
> *If I **lost** my job I **would go** abroad.*
>
> **Type 3**: *What would you have done if you had lost your job?*
> Asking/talking about imagined situations/consequences then:
> **'if' + past perfect + 'would have'**
> *If I **had lost** my job I **would have gone** abroad.*

Longman English Grammar Alexander

1 Which types express unreal (i.e. hypothetical) conditions?
2 What is significant about the *form* of these 'unreal' types?

2 Look back at the song lyrics in A and identify:

a one example of each of the three types
b any sentences that don't fit any of the types
c the pattern that they do follow

C Related forms

Study the following extract and answer the questions.

1 Which conditional pattern does the structure in exercise 2 have most in common with? Consider the form and meaning.
2 Which conditional pattern does the structure in exercises 4, 5 and 6 have most in common with? Consider the form and meaning.

2 🔊 Here is a list of regrets. Practise saying the sentences. Then choose three regrets that you share, and add two or more of your own.

I wish I had been nicer to my parents when I was younger.
I wish my family had had more money when I was small.
I wish I had listened to my mother's advice.
I wish I had worked harder at school when I was younger.
I wish I had gone to a different school.
I wish I had stayed at school for longer.
I wish I had left school earlier.
I wish I had not started learning English.
If only I had saved more money when I was younger!
If only I had travelled more when I was younger!
If only I had taken a different job!
If only I had not got married!
If only I had been born more beautiful!
If only I had been born more intelligent!
If only I had looked after my teeth better!
If only I had never started smoking!
If only I had gone to bed earlier last night!

4 Here are some wishes for the present or future. Choose three that you share, and add one or more.

I wish it was cooler/warmer.
I wish it was the end of the lesson.
I wish I was at home.
I wish I could sing / play the guitar.
I wish I had more money/time.
If only I spoke better English!
If only I knew more people!
If only people were more honest!
If only the government would do something about unemployment!
If only somebody would write me a letter!

5 Write your most important wish on a piece of paper, but without your name. Give it to the teacher.

6 Work in groups. The teacher will read out all the class's wishes to you. Write them down and divide them into different kinds of wish (e.g. wishes for material things; wishes for changes in one's situation). Report to the class: how many kinds of wish have you found, and what is the commonest kind of wish? What did you feel was the most surprising wish?

New Cambridge English Course 4 Swan, Walter and O'Sullivan

D Learner problems

Study these examples of learner errors. In each case, decide what the learner is getting wrong.

a If it will rain, we will wait for you in the house.
b If you didn't like it, you went!
c If I could choose a city to live in, I'm sure I'll choose Florence.
d If Cleopatra would have been ugly, history had been different.
e I wish I have more money!
f If only you didn't lose your passport! Now we will miss the plane.

E Functions and contexts

1 Complete the table.

Model sentence	Type	Likely function	Possible context
If you're not careful, you'll cut yourself.	1	warning	parent to child who is playing with scissors
I would've called you if I'd known you were ill.			
If I were you, I'd join a gym.			
If you like romance, you'll love this film.			
I'd live in the town centre if I could afford it.			
If you need anything, just help yourself.			
If you'd been here on time, we wouldn't have missed the flight.			

Language functions are dealt with in Unit 33.

2 Work in groups. Your trainer will assign you one of the model sentences in activity E1. Think of a way of presenting it so that its meaning and form are clear. Include these stages:

  • conveying the meaning
  • highlighting the form
  • checking understanding
  • providing initial practice

F Coursebooks

Study the coursebook you are using with your teaching practice classes. Find the section where it deals with conditional patterns and other ways of expressing hypothetical meaning, and answer the following questions.

1 What types are taught?
2 How do the books contextualise them?
3 How are they practised?
4 What information about the grammar is given to the learner? Is it clear? Is it similar to the information in section B, above?
5 Is this material appropriate for your learners?

REFLECTION

Work in groups of three. Discuss these questions.

a Rather than three conditional types (plus zero), some grammar books suggest a two-way division, between *real* and *unreal* conditions. Do you think such a division might be more user friendly?
b What do you think a 'mixed conditional' is? Can you think of an example?
c 'Conditional structures are typically formed with modal verbs.' Is this true?

33 Language functions

Warm-up

1 Match the captions with the cartoons.

1 ©Naf/www.CartoonStock.com

2 ©Ed McLachlan/ www.CartoonStock.com

3 ©Ed McLachlan/ www.CartoonStock.com

4 ©Ralph Hagen/ www.CartoonStock.com

5 ©Vahan Shirvanian/ www.CartoonStock.com

6 ©Noel Ford/ www.CartoonStock.com

    a *Well, my advice to you is to get a less powerful sports car.*
    b *Please turn it down – Daddy's trying to do your homework.*
    c *Sorry we're late, we had trouble finding you.*
    d *A virus ate my homework.*
    e *I'm watching you.*
    f *Tell Luigi to be a little more careful with the pepper.*

2 Identify the forms of the verbs in the captions. For example:

    a present simple of the verb *to be* and past simple of the verb *to have*.

3 Look at the cartoons and their captions again and answer these questions:

    a What is the context of each utterance? (i.e. where are the speakers and what are they are talking about?)
    b What is the relationship between the speaker and the person (or people) spoken to?

B Context and function

Every message has a purpose: this is called its (*communicative*) *function*. For example, a 'no smoking' sign functions as a prohibition, whereas a 'danger' sign functions as a warning.

1 Work in pairs. identify the functions of the utterances in A1.

2 Identify the cartoon captions where the choice of language makes the function explicit.

3 Discuss how you were able to infer the speaker's intention where the function was not explicit.

4 Look at the situations below where the same sentence is spoken in four different contexts. Decide on the function of the sentence in each case.

'It's ten past nine.'

a

b

c

d

5 Think of two different possible contexts and two corresponding functions for each of the following utterances.

    a I'll call the police.
    b It's cold in here.
    c That's the telephone.
    d Can you drive?

C Function, style and language

1 The choice between one of several different ways of performing a language function depends on a number of *context* factors. These factors will include such things as whether the message is spoken or written. Another key factor is the relationship between the people involved, such as how well they know each other, or the social distance between them. Decide on suitable utterances for the contexts described in the table.

Function	Context and utterance
inviting	a Write a short note inviting your new neighbours for a welcome drink at your house. b You want to have a drink with your friend after work. You say: ' …
asking a favour	c You want to borrow your flatmate's umbrella. You say: '… d You can't pick up your child from playschool today. You phone the parent of another child who attends the same playschool and leave an answerphone message, asking them to pick up your child. You say: ' …
making a suggestion	e Your local library has no DVD lending service. Write a short note on the subject for the library's suggestion box. f A work colleague is suffering from back pain, which you think is caused by the way their computer is positioned. You say: '…

There are particular ways of expressing many functions that have become conventionalised. For example, *Would you like [an X]?* typically functions as an offer. These *functional exponents* are often included in syllabuses, alongside grammar items.

2 Put the functional exponents in their correct place in this extract from an elementary syllabus.

Functions	Exponents
asking permission	1
polite requests	2
apologising and making excuses	3
asking for and giving opinions	4

C Language awareness

Functional exponents
a What was X like?
b Could you ...., please?
c I had to ....
d Can I ..., please?
e I thought it was ....
f I'm sorry I didn't ....

3 Work in pairs. Study the coursebook you are using with your teaching practice class. Find the syllabus for the course, which is usually located at the front of the book. Does it include ways of expressing different functions ('functional exponents')?

D Classroom application

Work in groups. Your trainer will assign each group a language function (such as *apologising*) and a level (such as *beginners*). With your group, create a short lesson as follows:

- Think of two situations in which the function might typically occur, one more formal than the other.
- Choose an appropriate way of expressing this function for each of the two situations.
- Write two short dialogues (6–8 lines) which contextualise the functional exponents you have chosen.
- Work out how you would use these dialogues to present and contrast the functional exponents to a class at the relevant level.

Be prepared to demonstrate your lesson to the rest of the class.

REFLECTION

The *functional approach* to language teaching emerged as a reaction to a purely *formal approach* – that is, the teaching of grammar forms or structures irrespective of the way they are used.

Work in groups of three. Discuss the answers to these questions.

a What sort of problems might a learner encounter who had been taught only language forms and not their associated functions?
b On the other hand, what might be the drawbacks of organising a course solely around language functions?
c Can you think of specific instances in your own experience, either as a second language user or as a teacher, where communication was impaired because of *inappropriate* (rather than *inaccurate*) language use?

34 The noun phrase

A Warm-up

1   Play the memory game *I went to market*. Your trainer will explain how.

2   Work in pairs. Discuss the benefits of a game like this.

3   Discuss how you could adapt the game for other language areas, such as *My X's Y*, as in *My brother's wife*, or *The X of Y*, as in *The Queen of England*.

B Noun types

1   Read this extract from a book and find an example of each of the items listed (a–i). Some are already done to help you.

> In the previous chapter we looked at the various roles that a teacher is called upon to fulfil. In this chapter we are going to look at two of these roles, 'organiser' and 'controller', in some detail. Being able to organise a class is every bit as important as understanding the nature of language or how languages may be learned. Without basic classroom management skills any lesson can quickly degenerate into chaos. One of the most important skills a teacher needs to develop is how to grade their own language so that it is appropriate to the class they are teaching. Having considered this, we will then go on to look at one of the biggest concerns for most new teachers, the issue of controlling the class. We will conclude the chapter by briefly looking at how common technological aids can be exploited effectively in the classroom.

Learning to Teach English Watkins

a   a singular noun, e.g. *chapter*
b   a plural noun, e.g. *roles*
c   a countable noun, i.e. a noun that refers to something that is considered to be a unit and so may have both singular and plural forms
d   an uncountable noun, i.e. a noun that refers to something that is thought of as being more like a mass or a substance and therefore doesn't normally have a plural form
e   a pronoun
f   an adjective that goes immediately before a noun and describes or identifies the noun
g   a noun that goes immediately before another noun and classifies that noun
h   a clause that comes immediately after a noun and serves to define or identify that noun, e.g. *that a teacher is called upon to fulfil*.
i   at least four different determiners, i.e. words that go before a noun and identify it or quantify it in some way

2 Read these extracts from the text. For each extract, decide how the meanings of the underlined words differ.

a
> ... understanding the nature of <u>language</u> or how <u>languages</u> may be learned.

b
> Being able to organise <u>a class</u> ... it is appropriate to <u>the class</u> they are teaching ... the issue of controlling <u>the class</u>

3 Read these examples of noun phrases (NPs) taken from the text. Use them to try to work out the principles of construction of the NP in English. It might help if you ask yourself the following questions:

* What element do all these noun phrases have in common?
* What optional elements can go before and after this common element?

a the previous chapter
b a teacher
c the nature of language
d basic classroom management skills
e chaos
f the class they are teaching
g one of the biggest concerns for most new teachers
h common technological aids

Phrase structure is also dealt with in Unit 27.

C Learners' problems

1 Decide which NP rule the learner is not applying correctly in these examples.
  a She has many friend.
  b Ted drives a lorry very big and fast.
  c I need some informations about this school.
  d My sister has got a long blond hair.
  e Can you give me a timetable of trains, please?
  f Excuse me, where is the buses station?
  g There is a carpet on the room's floor.
  h Do you have some brothers and sisters?
  i I like the ice cream and the bananas very much.
  j Most of Canadians speak a few French.
  k I am the student which arrive late.

2 Work in pairs. Your trainer will assign you some of the above errors. Assume that they occurred during controlled speaking activities and decide on an appropriate correction strategy in each case.

D Classroom application

1 Study the following coursebook exercises. Identify the aspect of the noun phrase that each one targets.

A

2 *Building language*

A 🎧 Listen. Find Rosa's roommate and Rosa's brother in the picture. Practice the conversation.

Jason So, is your new roommate here?
Rosa Yeah, she's right over there.
Jason Oh, which one is she?
Rosa She's the woman standing by the table.
Jason The one with short hair?
Rosa No, the woman with the ponytail.
Jason Oh, she looks nice. And who's that guy talking to her? He looks kind of weird.
Rosa You mean the guy in the yellow pants? That's my brother Jimmy.

Figure
it out → **B** Can you complete these sentences about the picture?

1. Rosa's the woman _____ the curly hair.
2. Jason's the guy _____ next to Rosa.
3. Jimmy's the guy _____ the yellow pants.

Touchstone 2 McCarthy, McCarten and Sandiford

B

3 Write three interesting statements, each of which combines a word from box A with a word from box B. Discuss your statements with a partner and the rest of your class.

For example:
Time is more important than money.   Men are a mystery to women.

A			
time	youth	wisdom	health
death	men	gold	music
war	humour		

+

B			
life	money	experience	love
women	peace	silver	
happiness	intelligence		

Inside Out (Upper-Intermediate) Kay and Jones

C Language awareness

C

● **Grammar question**

– When do we use **much** and when do we use **many**?

3 | **T.10** | Read and listen to the conversation between Ben and Sam.

Ben Now, have we got everything we need?
Sam Well, let's see. There are some onions and potatoes, but there aren't any mushrooms and, of course, there isn't any minced beef.
Ben Are there any carrots?
Sam A few. But we don't need many, so that's OK.
Ben How much milk is there?
Sam Only a little. And there isn't any butter, and we haven't got much cheese.
Ben Well, we don't need much cheese. Is there anything else?
Sam No, not for Shepherd's Pie. We've got some salt and pepper, and there's a lot of flour. Would you like me to help with the shopping?
Ben Yes, please.

Headway (Pre-Intermediate) Soars and Soars

D

4 Writing

1 Close your eyes and imagine a house just before a party.

2 Write a list of things you can see, hear and smell.

3 In groups, write a poem called 'Before the party'. Use patterns like these:

A lot of people running
Some baked potatoes
A few packets of crisps
Not much time

The Intermediate Choice Mohamed and Acklam

2 Identify which of the coursebook exercises in A–D above are presentation and which are practice activities.

3 Work in pairs. Decide how you would follow up each presentation element in class.

REFLECTION

1 Underline the noun phrases in this text. The first two have been done for you.

> Adjusting <u>your language</u> for <u>the level of the learners you are teaching</u> can be very difficult, but is a very important teaching skill. It is important that the models you give learners remain reasonably natural because learners will pick these up. The language which it is appropriate to use with a low level class will be significantly different from the language used with a higher class, although it should remain natural. It is not necessary that learners understand every word you say …

Learning to Teach English Watkins

2 Decide how each noun phrase that you have underlined is constructed and complete the table below. The first one has been done for you.

Pre-modification	Head	Post-modification
your	language	

3 Read the transcript of what a trainer actually said and answer the questions.

'You need to make sure you grade your language especially when you're teaching beginners and elementary groups. This doesn't mean speaking baby talk because erm you should still try and speak at a natural pace, and not, you know, simplify your language, I mean not to the point that it becomes like pidgin or sort of ungrammatical. But at the same time you have to choo …, you should try and choose your words quite carefully, and use gestures and so on to make it really clear what you mean …'

a How does the use of noun phrases differ in the written and the spoken texts?
b What does this suggest about the teaching of this area of grammar?

35 The sounds of English

A Warm-up

1 Your trainer is going to give you a 'new name'. Memorise your name, but keep it secret. Your trainer will call the class register. When you hear your name say 'Present'.

2 Think about these questions.
   1 What problems might learners of English have with this activity? Why?
   2 What aspect of language does the activity target?

B Sounds vs letters

1 Write down the words your trainer dictates. Then check your spelling with a partner.

2 Work in pairs. Discuss the meanings of these words and see if you agree on them.

3 Count the letters and the sounds in each word. For example:
   letter = six letters (L-E-T-T-E-R) and four sounds (l-e-tt-er)

4 Work in pairs. Discuss what activity B3 demonstrates about the sound–spelling relationship in English.

C Consonant sounds

1 Consonant sounds are formed when the airflow from the lungs is obstructed by the moveable parts of the mouth, including the tongue and lips. Try pronouncing these sounds, and decide where the obstruction is occurring.

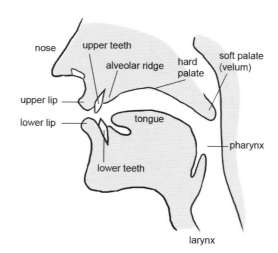

For example, the sound /b/ (as in *ban*) is articulated by obstructing the airflow at the lips.

/m/ as in *man*
/v/ as in *van*
/n/ as in *nan*
/t/ as in *tan*
/r/ as in *ran*
/k/ as in *can*

Because of the mismatch between spelling and sound, it is necessary to use a special script (called *phonemic script*) to transcribe spoken language. Here is a list that shows the 24 consonant sounds of standard British English in phonemic script.

p	p̲en	b	b̲in
t	t̲in	d	d̲id
tʃ	ch̲in	dʒ	gentle
k	k̲id	g	get
f	f̲in	v	v̲ent
θ	th̲in	ð	th̲ese
s	s̲at	z	z̲one
ʃ	sh̲irt	ʒ	pleas̲ure
m	m̲en	n	n̲ib
ŋ	wi̲ng̲	h	h̲en
l	l̲et	r	r̲ed
w	w̲e	j	y̲et (written as **y** in North American English phonemic script)

Many of the consonants consist of *voiceless* and *voiced* pairs, such as /p/ and /b/. A *voiced* sound is one that is made by activating the *vocal cords*. (You can feel them vibrate if you put your hand on your throat.) To produce a *voiceless* sound, no vocal cord activation is required.

2 Read these words using the list above.

a /met/   b /dek/   c /ðen/   d /hedʒ/   e /breθ/   f /fetʃ/   g /nekst/   h /jet/
i /ʃred/   j /ʃrɪŋk/

3 Write these words in phonemic script.

a sent   b edge   c thin   d thing   e think   f this   g fixed   h jest   i yelled   j stretched

D Vowel sounds

Vowels are formed, not by obstructing the airflow, but by modifying its passage through the mouth, principally through the use of the tongue and lips. Vowels are divided between *monophthongs* (single vowels) and *diphthongs* (a glide from one vowel to another). All vowels are voiced, that is, they involve activating the vocal cords. The vowel sound /ə/ is so frequent in English that it has its own name: *schwa*. It is the unstressed, neutral vowel sound at the end of words like *sister*, for example, or at the beginning of words like *ago*. On the left are listed the vowels of standard British English in phonemic script. On the right are listed the vowels of North American English.

British English			
iː	we	ɪə	dear
ɪ	fit	eɪ	say
ʊ	look	ʊə	sure
uː	hoot	ɔɪ	toy
e	fed	əʊ	so
ə	a̲lone	eə	fair
ɜː	hurt	aɪ	die
ɔː	ought	aʊ	how
æ	hat		
ʌ	but		
ɑː	tar		
ɒ	pot		

American English			
iy	we	ey	say
ɪ	fit	ɔy	toy
ʊ	foot	ow	so
uw	hoot	ay	die
e	fed	ɑw	how
ə	a̲lone		
ɜʳ	hurt		
ɔ	ought		
æ	hat		
ʌ	but		
ɑ	fa̲ther, pot		

C Language awareness

1 Decipher these film titles using the consonant chart and the vowel chart.

British English

a /bætmæn/   f /saɪkəʊ/
b /kɪŋ kɒŋ/   g /jʌŋ fræŋkənstaɪn/
c /eəpleɪn/   h /ʃɪkɑːgəʊ/
d /dʒɔːz/   i /dɒktə ʒɪvɑːgəʊ/
e /ðə bɜːdz/   j /dʒɔːz tuː/

American English

a /bætmæn/   f /saykow/
b /kɪŋ kɑŋ/   g /yʌŋ fræŋkənstayn/
c /erpleyn/   h /ʃɪkagow/
d /dʒɔz/   i /daktərʳ ʒɪvagow/
e /ðə bɜʳdz/   j /dʒɔz tuw/

2 Write these film titles in phonemic script.

a Shrek   b Ben Hur   c Snatch   d Star Wars   e High Noon   f Blade Runner
g Memento   h Mystic River

3 Work in pairs. Write two more film titles in phonemic script for your partner to decipher.

E Sounds in connected speech

Sounds are seldom produced in isolation. In *connected speech* (that is, any sequence of words spoken at natural speed), many sounds tend to be altered or modified by the sounds immediately before or after them, especially at the boundaries between words.

1 Read these film titles aloud and notice what happens to the sounds in the underlined segment when you say the title at a natural speed.

a The La<u>st P</u>icture Show
b My Big Fa<u>t G</u>reek Wedding
c The Grea<u>t D</u>ictator
d The Gree<u>n M</u>ile

e Sta<u>nd b</u>y your Man
f The Wa<u>r o</u>f the Worlds
g W<u>e a</u>re Family

2 Work in groups of three. Discuss why these connected speech effects might cause problems for learners.

F The phonemic chart

For teaching purposes, the sounds of English are often displayed in the form of a phonemic chart:

British English Phonemic Chart

iː	ɪ	ʊ	uː	ɪə	eɪ	✗
e	ə	ɜː	ɔː	ʊə	ɔɪ	əʊ
æ	ʌ	ɑː	ɒ	eə	aɪ	aʊ
p	b	t	d	tʃ	dʒ	k	g
f	v	θ	ð	s	z	ʃ	ʒ
m	n	ŋ	h	l	r	w	j

American English Phonemic Chart

iy	ɪ	ʊ	uw
ey	ə(r)	ow	ay
e	ɜʳ	ɔ	ɑw
æ	ʌ	ɑ	ɔy
p	b	t	d	tʃ	dʒ	k	g
f	v	θ	ð	s	z	ʃ	ʒ
m	n	ŋ	h	l	r	w	y

Sound Foundations Underhill

156

1 Read the three teaching techniques – A, B and C – that involve the use of this chart. In each case, answer these questions.

    a What is the purpose of the technique?

    b What do learners need to know in order for the technique to work?

Lesson A

The learners are doing a speaking exercise. One learner says, 'I leave in a small village'. The teacher says, 'Not *leave*', and points to the symbol /ɪ/ on the chart.

Lesson B

The teacher is teaching a set of words relating to transport. She holds up a picture of a van, and, using a pointer, she silently points to these symbols on the chart: /v/, /æ/, /n/. She then invites the learners to sound out the word.

Lesson C

The teacher holds up a picture of a pear and says the word *pear* while pointing to the symbol /p/ on the chart. She then holds up a picture of a bear, and says the word *bear* while pointing at the symbol /b/. The same process continues, using pictures for these words: *pin*, *bin*; *cap*, *cab*; *path*, *bath*; etc. and alternating between pointing at /p/ and pointing at /b/. She next asks the learners each to write /p/ and /b/ on two separate pieces of paper. She then says the words in a random order, and the students have to hold up the piece of paper that corresponds to the sound that they hear. For example, on hearing *cab*, they hold up /b/; on hearing *cap*, they hold up /p/.

---

2 Think of a group of learners that you are teaching or have taught and that share a mother tongue. Identify a pair of sounds – like /p/ and /b/ – that they easily confuse and that you might target using technique C above.

Teaching pronunciation is dealt with in Unit 37.

REFLECTION

Answer these questions.

a How many letters are there in English?

b How many sounds are there?

c What's the difference between a consonant sound and a vowel sound?

d What's the difference between the sound /s/ and the sound /z/?

e What's the name of the most common vowel sound in English?

f What's the difference between the sound /ɪ/ in *pin* and the sound /aɪ/ in *pine*?

g What sound do these three words have in common: *does, zoo, noise*?

h What sound do these three words have in common: *first, surf, earns*?

i True or false? /ʃeɪkspɪə rəʊt məkbeθ/

j True or false? /njuː jɔːk ɪz ɪn teksəs/

36 Stress, rhythm and intonation

A Warm-up

1 Work in pairs. Do the activity and discuss what it demonstrates.

> **Imagine you are in a bar or café, and you've both just finished a drink, or a slice of chocolate cake. Have a conversation in which you use only the word 'Well'. The conversation should convey these meanings:**
>
> A: That was nice!
> B: Shall we have another one?
> A: I shouldn't really.
> B: I'm going to have another one, even if you're not.
> A: If you're going to insist …
> B: You're easily convinced – you surprise me!

2 Discuss whether learners would find this activity easy or difficult. Give reasons for your opinion.

B Stress

Stress is the prominence that is given to particular syllables (in a word) or to particular words (in an utterance).

1 Work in pairs. Read these invented words and try to predict the way that each one is stressed. Decide what the results of this exercise suggest about the rules of word stress in English.

pawler   veddle   malmish   pandiful   loomitive   loomition   imbelist   imbelistic
geon   geonics   geonetics   geonetology   geonetological

2 Identify six to eight vocabulary items relating to a particular theme (such as jobs, food and drink, clothing, etc.) in the coursebook you are currently using with your teaching practice class. Then answer the questions.

   1 Which is the stressed syllable in each of these words?
   2 What techniques could you use to highlight the stress?

3 Work in pairs. Read these short dialogues aloud, taking turns to read sentences A and B. Then answer the questions.

   A: Let's invite Jack to dinner next Saturday.
   B: No, let's invite Jack to dinner next Friday.

   A: Let's invite Jack to dinner next Saturday.
   B: No, let's invite Jill to dinner next Saturday.

   A: Let's invite Jack to dinner next Saturday.
   B: No, let's invite Jack to lunch next Saturday.

   A: Let's invite Jack to dinner next Saturday.
   B: No, let's not invite Jack to dinner next Saturday.

1   In what way does the second sentence change?
2   Why does the sentence change in this way?

4   Work in pairs or groups of three. Write a short dialogue (6–8 lines) between two people who have just been introduced at a party. Include at least one example of an utterance that is repeated by another speaker, but with a change of stress. Mark the main stressed word in each utterance.

5   Decide how you could use this dialogue in class.

C   Rhythm

1   Work in pairs. Take turns to read aloud the following sentences so that each sentence takes the same number of beats as the first sentence (which you should read fairly slowly and deliberately). It may help to beat the rhythm with your hand. Then answer the questions.

■	■	■
Words	take	stress.
Words	take	stress.
Words should	take	stress.
Words should	take	stress.
Words should	take the	stress.
Words should	take the	stress.
Some words should	take the	stress.
Some words should	take the	stress.
Some words should've	taken the	stress.
Some words should've	taken the	stress.
Some of the words should've	taken the	stress.
Some of the words should've	taken the	stress.

1   What happens to the individual words as the sentence becomes longer?
2   Why might this create a problem for students – in terms of both listening and speaking?

2   Study this coursebook activity, and decide what aspect of pronunciation it targets.

3   Work in pairs. Discuss how this aspect of pronunciation might be connected with rhythm.

3   Remember that some words have two pronunciations: a 'weak form' and a 'strong form'. Examples:

	MUST	CAN	HAVE	WAS
WEAK:	/ms, məst/	/kn, kən/	/(h)əv/	/w(ə)z/
STRONG:	/mʌst/	/kæn/	/hæv/	/wɒz/

Which pronunciation do *must*, *can*, *have* and *was* have in these sentences? Write W (weak) or S (strong). Don't worry about negatives – they're always strong.

1. Of course she must.
2. I think I must phone my mother today.
3. I can't come today, but I can tomorrow.
4. When can we leave?
5. I wonder where the twins have gone.
6. We haven't lost Ted, have we?
7. I think I'll have a shower.
8. That *was* a nice dinner. Thank you so much.
9. Yes, she was.

New Cambridge English Course 3 Swan, Walter and O'Sullivan

159

D Intonation

1 Work in pairs. Say each of the following pairs of sentences aloud in two different ways, paying attention to the punctuation and other non-verbal signs. Then answer the questions.

1 What is the difference in meaning?

2 How is this difference conveyed?

For example:

I like Chinese art and opera. I like |Chinese art and opera| (= Chinese art and Chinese opera)

I like Chinese art, and opera. I like |Chinese art| and opera| (= Chinese art and any kind of opera)

a (1) The people who left suddenly – started running.

   (2) The people who left – suddenly started running.

b (1) My brother who lives in New York has a penthouse.

   (2) My brother, who lives in New York, has a penthouse.

c (1) She didn't marry him – because of his parents.

   (2) She didn't marry him because of his PARENTS …

d (1) You're a nurse.

   (2) You're a nurse?

e (1) Dan's not English, is he!?

   (2) Dan's not English, is he?

f (1) (*What's the capital of Mexico?*) Mexico City.

   (2) (*What's the capital of Mexico?*) Mexico City?

g (1) We need eggs sugar milk butter.

   (2) We need eggs sugar milk butter …

h (1) Hi!!!!!

   (2) Hi.

i (1) Thanks a lot. ☹

   (2) Thanks a lot. ☺

2 In the light of the above exercise, decide what effects changes in intonation have.

3 Work with a partner. Discuss ways in which problems with intonation might prejudice communication.

4 Study the following two activities and decide what function of intonation each of them focuses on.

---

1 **Listen to these two short conversations. The words are exactly the same in both conversations, but in one Speaker A sounds polite, and in the other she doesn't. Can you tell which is which? What is the difference?**

A: What's your name?
B: James.
A: Your full name?
B: James Haddon.
A: What nationality are you?
B: Australian.
A: Why do you want a visa?
B: For tourism.

Now, practise saying the dialogue in the polite way.

2 **Listen to these questions. In which questions does the person who is asking the question a) *know* the answer; b) *not know* the answer?**

a You're married, aren't you?
b You're married, aren't you?
c It's not raining again, is it?
d It's a lovely day, isn't it?
e You'll phone, won't you?
f You won't be late, will you?

Now, practise saying the following questions in two ways …

REFLECTION

Discuss these questions in pairs or groups.

a Which of the following areas do you think is most critical in ensuring communicative effectiveness? Why?
    i   accurate production of individual sounds (i.e. vowels and consonants)
    ii   accurate stress placement in words
    iii accurate stress placement in utterances
    iv   accurate production of strong and weak forms
    v   native-like rhythm
    vi   accurate use of intonation
b Which of the above areas do you think is the most easily learnable? Why?

37 Teaching pronunciation

A Warm-up

1 Study these learner errors. Identify the area of pronunciation that each of them relates to.

	Learner pronunciation	Correct version
a	Our president is very IMportant.	Our president is very imPORtant.
b	It is bad to heat children.	It is bad to hit children.
c	It's a nice day, isn't it? ⟶	It's a nice day, isn't it ⟶
d	Who are you waiting FOR?	Who are you WAITING for?
e	How many beeble live there?	How many people live there?
f	IF ONLY I HAD KNOWN!	If only I'd KNOWN!

2 Work with a partner. Discuss these statements and decide to what extent you agree.

   a The best model for teaching pronunciation is RP (*Received Pronunciation*, i.e. the regionally neutral, prestige accent of Britain).
   b Mispronunciation of individual sounds (the 'small' features) is less important than errors at the level of stress, intonation and rhythm ('big' features).
   c It is hard to unlearn incorrect habits; therefore it is important to get pronunciation right as soon as possible.
   d Intelligibility (i.e. being understood) is more important than sounding like a native speaker.
   e One of the best ways of teaching pronunciation is always to speak naturally to the learners.

B Pronunciation exercises

1 Study the pronunciation activities below and answer the questions.

   1 What aspect of pronunciation is each activity targeting? Is it a 'small' feature (such as individual sounds) or a 'big' feature (such as sentence stress or intonation)?
   2 Is the objective of the activity *reception* or *production* (or both)?
   3 Is the feature used in context or is it decontextualised?
   4 How *communicative* is the activity? Could non-communicative activities be adapted to make them more communicative?

   a
   > The teacher demonstrates the difference in the pronunciation of the *-ed* ending on *worked*, *lived* and *started*. She then asks students to make three columns in their books, headed by /t/, /d/ and /ɪd/ respectively. She reads out a list of past tense words, e.g. *opened*, *walked*, *moved*, *lifted*, *missed*, *waited* etc.; the students write each one in the appropriate column.

b

> The teacher prepares cards of rhyming words, e.g. *steak, make; do, true*, etc. In groups, students take turns to table the cards; if a card rhymes with the preceding card, the player keeps the pair. The winner is the player with the most pairs.

c

> The teacher tells a story that the students know, making deliberate mistakes, which the class have to correct. For example:
> T: Little Red Riding Hood lived in a cottage in the middle of a desert.
> L: No, she lived in the middle of a *wood*.
> T: Oh, yes, she lived near a wood.
> L: No, *in* a wood...

The Pronunciation Book Bowen and Marks

d

> The teacher prepares cards on which are written different quantities of money, e.g. 5 cents; 50 cents; 5 dollars; 50 dollars; 500 dollars, etc. She hands individual students the cards, saying 'Here's a present for you'. The students should respond by saying 'Thank you' in a way that is proportionate to the amount of the gift.

e

> The teacher sets up a speaking exercise, e.g. dialogue, role play, chat, etc. When students make a mistake in their pronunciation, the teacher acts 'dumb', e.g. she says, or indicates, 'I'm sorry, I don't understand'. The student tries to correct him/herself.

f

> The teacher plays a short section (one sentence or less) of recorded speech, and leaves a few moments' silence to allow the sound of the words to register. The students are asked to echo the segment internally, without speaking. The teacher replays the segment. This time, the students 'subvocalise', i.e. repeat the segment under their breath. Next the students are asked to speak aloud and in step with the recording ('shadowing'). The segment is repeated a number of times and then a new segment is attempted.

The Pronunciation Book Bowen and Marks

2 Work in groups. Evaluate the activities in B1. For example, discuss whether, as a learner, *you* would like to do them. Decide whether you think they would improve your pronunciation. Give reasons.

Anticipating problems

1 Work in pairs. Discuss the pronunciation problems learners might have with these syllabus areas.

a *can/can't* (to talk about ability)
(Possible problem: failure to discriminate between weak and strong forms, so that *can* sounds like *can't* ...)
b ordinal numbers, i.e. *first, second, third, fourth*, etc.
c *used to* (to talk about past habits)
d present simple questions, e.g. *Where does she live? What do you do?*

C Language awareness

    e polite requests using *would you mind … -ing?*

    f clothing vocabulary, e.g. *shirt, shorts, suit, shoes, jacket, coat, scarf*, etc.

2 Your trainer will assign you one of the above areas. Think of classroom solutions to the problems that students might have. For example:

    a *can/can't*

       Possible solution: the teacher repeats one of the words several times and then changes to the other word. Learners have to stop the teacher when they hear the change – *can can can can can't can't can't can't can*, etc. (Learners could then do this in pairs.)

D Classroom application

Study this extract from a coursebook (with its accompanying transcript). No explicit pronunciation work has been included. Decide where you think it would be appropriate to include some work on pronunciation and what form this could take.

Useful language

1 Look at these expressions in a clothes shop, and mark them **C** for customer and **A** for assistant.

Asking	Trying on	Paying
I'm just looking, thanks.	Could I try it / them on, please?	Can I pay by credit card?
Can I help you?	The fitting rooms are over there.	How would you like to pay?
What size would you like?	Any good?	Cash or credit card?
Have you got this in a size 12 / a medium?	It's a bit tight / big / small.	Your receipt's in the bag.
I'll just have a look.	Do you think I could try on a bigger one?	
I'll take it / them.		

2 🔲 **0.3** Listen to this dialogue and tick (✓) the expressions you hear.

3 Which expressions could be useful for buying other things?

4 Compare these two questions. Which is more polite?
Where are the CDs, please?   *Could you tell me where the CDs are, please?*

Practice

1 **Against the clock** ▩ 3 minutes ▩ Make these sentences more polite.

    1 I want to try it on.

    2 Where's the shampoo?

    3 Give me a phonecard.

    4 I want to pay by credit card.

    5 I want you to dry clean this suit today.

    6 How much is this?

    7 Give me a smaller one to try.

    8 Where are the fitting rooms?

2 🔲 **0.4** Listen and check your ideas. Repeat the sentences and try to sound exactly the same.

3 In pairs. Make short dialogues which include these phrases.

A Could I have a film for this camera, please?
B Would you like black and white or colour?
A Colour, please.

1 black and white or colour?
2 where the travel books are?
3 dry clean this jacket?
4 battery for my camera?
5 shirt costs?
6 I'm sorry, we haven't got any fitting rooms.
7 wash, cut, and blow dry.
8 24 aspirin?
9 film starts?

Assistant	Hello, can I help you?
Customer	Yes, have you got this in a size 12?
Assistant	In blue?
Customer	Yes, in blue.
Assistant	I'll just have a look. Yes, here you are.
Customer	Could I try it on, please?
Assistant	Of course. The fitting rooms are over there.
Customer	Thank you.

Assistant	Any good?
Customer	I think it's a bit tight. Do you think I could try on a bigger one?
Assistant	Yes, I'll see if we've got a 14.

Assistant	Better?
Customer	Yes, I'll take it.
Assistant	Great, OK, if you could take it to the cash desk.

Cashier	How would you like to pay?
Customer	Cash, please.
Cashier	That'll be 15.99, then.
Customer	There you are.
Cashier	16, 17, 18, 19, 20. Thanks. Your receipt's in the bag. Goodbye.
Customer	Thanks very much. Bye.

1 Could I try it on, please?
2 Can you tell me where the shampoo is?
3 I'd like to buy a phonecard, please.
4 Can I pay by credit card?
5 Could you possibly dry clean this suit today?
6 Could you tell me how much this is?
7 Can I try a smaller one, please?
8 Could you tell me where the fitting rooms are?

Clockwise (Pre-Intermediate) McGowen and Richardson

REFLECTION

1 Read these terms, which relate to the teaching of pronunciation. Check that you understand the meaning of them.
  • integrated
  • intelligible
  • communicative
  • receptive
  • accent
  • context
  • English as an International Language (EIL)
  • teachable
  • RP
2 Choose at least three of the terms and use each one in a sentence in order to sum up your own views on pronunciation teaching.
3 Compare your sentences in pairs or groups.

38 Vocabulary

A Warm-up

1 Work in pairs or groups. Brainstorm as many words as you can think of that relate to the topic of DIY (do-it-yourself). You have one minute.

2 Compare your words with those of another group. Identify how many you had that were the same and how many were different.

3 Decide if it is possible to make connections between any of your words. For example, if you had *tool* and *hammer*, you could say that *a hammer is a kind of tool*; *paint* and *brush* can combine to make *paintbrush*.

B Lexical meaning

Read the following text. Identify any words that you brainstormed in A. Then answer the questions.

Step class

If one of your nagging DIY jobs needs a ladder, bear in mind 50 people die and 40,000 need hospital treatment every year through domestic accidents involving ladders. The vast majority of victims are enthusiastic males. The Department of Trade and Industry is so concerned it produces *The Ladder User's Handbook*, available at most large DIY centres. Consider these ten points before you prop your steps up with the Yellow Pages:

1 Put the ladder on a firm, level, dry surface. On soft earth, bolster with a wooden board.
2 Position leaning ladders so the base won't slip outwards. Check the rubber feet are in good condition.
3 Rest the top of the ladder against a solid surface, not plastic guttering. Secure it with ropes tied from the stiles (ladder edges) to fixed objects or stakes in the ground.
4 Never stand on the top three rungs.
5 Don't reach too far sideways – climb down, untie the ladder, move and resecure it.
6 Use a shoulder-bag to carry equipment up and down.
7 Hold on to the ladder with one hand while you work. You can get a special tray to fix on the ladder for paint-pots and tools.
8 Wear shoes with dry soles and a good grip, not sandals, slip-ons or bare feet.
9 If you climb a ladder in front of a door, lock or block it first.
10 Don't use a ladder in strong winds or near power lines.

(from article in *Men's Health*)

a   What is the relation between the underlined words in each of these groups of words from the text? For example: *a wooden board*; *the rubber feet*; *plastic guttering* are related in the sense that they are specific *types of* a general class of things (*materials*).
    They are also the same word class (adjectives).
    i   the vast majority of victims; at most large DIY centres
    ii   bear in mind 50 people die; consider these ten points
    iii on a firm, level, dry, surface; On soft earth…
    iv   bear in mind; bare feet
    v   to fix on the ladder; to fixed objects
    vi   the vast majority; Trade and Industry; bare feet
    vii Wear shoes …, not sandals, slip-ons
    viii need hospital treatment … through domestic accidents; The vast majority of victims
b   'If one of your nagging DIY jobs …' How does this differ from 'If one of your persistent home improvement responsibilities …'?

C   Word formation

In English, new words can be formed by combining old ones – a process called 'compounding'; or by adding prefixes and suffixes (such as *pre-* or *-less*) – a process called 'affixation'. Some 'words' in fact comprise more than one word: they take the form of multi-word units (also called 'chunks'). Phrasal verbs are a kind of multi-word unit composed of a verb and a particle, e.g. *down, in, over*.

1   Match the modes of formation (1–4) with the examples from the text (a–d).

Mode of formation	Example from text
1 compounding (= putting two or more words together to make one)	a *prop … up, hold on, climb down*
2 affixation (= adding prefixes or suffixes)	b *handbook, shoulder-bag, paint-pots*
3 multi-word unit (chunk) (= two or more words that have one complete meaning)	c *untie, resecure; equipment, treatment*
4 phrasal verb (= verb plus particle, having one complete meaning)	d *bear in mind, in front of*

2   Identify the affix (i.e. the prefix or suffix) in each of the following words from the text. Then answer the questions.
    available   equipment   guttering   resecure   untie   user
    a   What is the basic meaning of the affix?
    b   Can you think of more examples of words with each affix?

D   Vocabulary focus

1   Study these three coursebook activities. Identify the aspect of word meaning or word formation that each one targets.

a

Wordspot

say and *tell*

1 Do we *say* or *tell* the following things? Write them in the correct diagram below. Spend a few minutes memorising the phrases:

a someone off
b the truth / lies
c someone to do something
d 'hello' / 'goodbye'
e 'thank you'
f someone about something

g 'yes' / 'no'
h you're sorry
i a prayer
j the difference between two things
k a story / joke
l someone what to do

'hello' / 'goodbye'

....
SAY
....
....
....

someone off

....
TELL
....
....
....
....
....

Cutting Edge (Intermediate) Cunningham and Moor

b

affixes

Certain prefixes and suffixes are often used to describe features of products.

affix	meaning	other examples
fat-<u>free</u> yoghurt	= no fat	sugar-free, alcohol-free
home-<u>made</u> bread	= made at home	hand-made
locally-<u>grown</u> fruit	= produced locally	home- / organically-grown
<u>non</u>-iron shirt	= you don't iron	non-stick, non-slip
a water-<u>proof</u> watch	= not damaged / affected by water	bullet-proof, sound-proof

1 What features could these products have?

a chocolates *hand-made chocolates*
b a raincoat
c cherries
d a recording studio

e beer
f cola
g frying pan
h shoes

2 What do the prefixes in bold mean?

mini-disc	**micro**film	**multi**-media	**pre**-cooked

3 Use your dictionary to find more examples for these prefixes.

Natural English (Upper-Intermediate) Gairns and Redman

c

2 | Slang

In the conversation you heard *pinch his wallet*. Match the slang words 1–8 to the neutral equivalents a–h

1 Chuck it to me.
2 Have you got a fag?
3 They went out boozing.
4 My bicycle's been nicked.
5 I've decided to flog the car.
6 It only cost ten quid.
7 He's a really nice bloke.
8 He flipped his lid.

a lost his temper
b stolen
c throw
d sell
e drinking
f cigarette
g pounds
h man

Innovations (Upper-Intermediate) Dellar, Hocking and Walkley

2 Work in pairs. Decide how you could follow up each of these activities in class.

Teaching vocabulary is dealt with in Unit 5.

E Lexical difficulty

1 Work in pairs. Decide which of these words taken from the text in B1 might cause learners difficulty in understanding. Give reasons.

bolster   equipment   fixed   hospital   nagging   prop up   stiles

2 Decide what problems learners might have in producing the above words (i.e. in using them in speaking or writing).

3 Choose up to five words in the text that you would pre-teach before giving the text to a class of upper-intermediate learners to read.

4 Discuss what factors determined your choice of words.

REFLECTION

Find a text (e.g. the text on page 124, or one in the coursebook you are using) and choose an area of vocabulary that you could focus on. For example, a lexical set, collocation, multi-word units, etc. How would you use the text for this purpose?

39 Text grammar

A Warm-up

1 Your trainer will give you the title of a text. Listen to the instructions and do the activity.

2 Read the text that has your sentence at the top and answer the questions.
   1 Does it make sense?
   2 Does it hold together?

3 Compare ideas with a partner.

B Connected text

1 Work in groups of three. Read the sentences and sort them into two texts.

1	Some prehistoric ferns were as tall as trees.
2	The male grasshopper chirps to attract a mate.
3	They live in fields and meadows and feed on green plants.
4	The wind scatters the spores on to the ground and they grow into tiny plants.
5	**GRASSHOPPER**
6	Ferns have no flowers or seeds.
7	Grasshoppers are insects.
8	He does this by rubbing the insides of his back legs against his wings.
9	Later these plants grow into new ferns.
10	Ferns are primitive plants.
11	**FERN**
12	Instead they have tiny cells called spores under their leaves.
13	They can hop as much as 75 centimetres.
14	There have been ferns on Earth for over 300 million years.

(adapted from *Pocket Encyclopedia* Jack)

2 Now order the sentences within each text.

3 Your trainer will give you a copy of the two texts. Check that your own versions match the originals. If not, account for any differences.

4 Work in pairs. Discuss what kinds of knowledge you drew on to be able to separate the texts and to order them.

C Cohesion

1   Read these sentences. Explain why it is unlikely that any of them could be the first sentence of a text.

> a   They live in fields and meadows and feed on green plants.
> b   Instead they have tiny cells called spores under their leaves.
> c   Later these plants grow into new ferns.
> d   He does this by rubbing the insides of his back legs against his wings.
> e   The wind scatters the spores on to the ground and they grow into tiny plants.

(adapted from *Pocket Encyclopedia* Jack)

2   Decide why a learner might think that these pairs of sentences were connected.

> a   They live in fields and meadows and feed on green plants. Later these plants grow into new ferns.
> b   Ferns have no flowers or seeds. They can hop as much as 75 centimetres.

(adapted from *Pocket Encyclopedia* Jack)

3   Read the text and identify at least four different ways in which its sentences are linked. Then answer the questions.

> **COPPER**
> Copper was one of the first metals to be used. To begin with, people used pure copper which they found on the ground. But they later learned how to extract it from ore by smelting.
> Pure copper is very soft. It is often mixed with other metals to make a harder alloy like brass.

(*Pocket Encyclopedia* Jack)

1   Which of these ways of linking sentences are lexical (i.e. to do with words)?
2   Which are more grammatical?

4   Read this summary of the main lexical and grammatical ways a text can be made cohesive. Then study the two coursebook exercises and decide which aspects of cohesion each one focuses on.

Lexical

* repetition of words, or words from the same word family (e.g. *copper – copper; metal – metallic*) or use of synonyms
* use of general words to refer to something more specific that is mentioned elsewhere (e.g. *grasshopper – the insect*)
* use of topically related words (e.g. *copper, ore, brass, alloy*)
* substitution of previously mentioned words with *one/ones* or *none*: *Some plants have flowers. Ferns have none.*
* ellipsis of previously mentioned words (i.e. leaving a word out because it can be recovered from the previous text, as in *Insects have six legs. Spiders have eight [legs].*)

Grammatical

* reference devices, especially pronouns (*people – they; it does this*)
* substitution of previously mentioned clause elements, with *do/does* or *did*, or *so/not: Spiders don't have wings. Most insects do.*
* linkers, such as *therefore, what's more, then*

8 | Writing: connecting ideas

I Put these sentences in order to complete the text.

a Finally, and most importantly perhaps, does long life really mean happiness? ....

b And then there's the question of who decides who's going to live or die? ....

c In other words, a good life, if not always a long one. ....*8*....

d In the first place, there are already too many people in the world. ....

e On the contrary, all I ask is that we should be concentrating on improving the quality of life, not its quantity. ....

f Don't think, however, that I am arguing for a return to the Middle Ages. ....

g Let me say from the start that I don't agree with the idea that life should be artificially prolonged. ......*1*......

h Secondly, who's going to pay to support a population of aged people? ....

2 Underline all the words or expressions used to connect ideas.

The Intermediate Choice (*Workbook*) Thornbury

With a partner, use reference words from the box to replace the underlined words.

This   They   He   She   Them   It   These

1 We need to make an effort to understand how things work in other cultures. The effort is the first step to effective communication across cultures.

2 Many presenters like to use gestures. Gestures help the audience to follow the flow of a presentation.

3 Using idioms in a presentation can cause trouble. Idioms can sometimes have two meanings.

4 I had a conversation with a Malaysian woman. The Malaysian woman told me a story about a presentation that went wrong.

Business Explorer 2 Knight and O'Neil

D Coherence

1 Read the text below and decide what is wrong with it.

METAL

Copper was one of the first metals to be used. Many metals have a silvery, shiny surface. But most of the dyes used these days are made from chemicals. They can hop as much as 75 centimetres. Others, such as the cockle, use their single foot to move around. Most non-metals do not.

(adapted from *Pocket Encyclopedia* Jack)

2 The way that a text is organised contributes to its general coherence. Read the text below and compare it with the *Fern* text from section B. Then answer the questions.

MOLLUSCS

Molluscs are animals with soft bodies. To protect themselves, many molluscs have shells.

Some molluscs, like the mussel, stay inside their shells and hardly ever move. Others, such as the cockle, use their single foot to move around. Snails and slugs crawl very slowly.

(*Pocket Encyclopedia* Jack)

1 How do the texts both begin?
2 How is the second paragraph of each one different from the first?
3 Can you generalise some *generic* features of this type of text? (You can refer to the *copper* text, too.)

E Classroom application

1 Read this example of learner writing and answer the questions.

Dear Sir,

I would like to express you what is my opinion about the programmes you are showing through our local TV Channel. I supose you are not psicologist, you are 'only' a manager, but I think any person should know that TV is a mass-media you should use to release information, entertainment, culture, or anything like this. But you did not get it, and you use TV as a gun, as a weapon, trying to scare everyone who lays in his comfortable sofa, waiting for an only acceptable TV programme just to spend the last few day hours relaxed.

In the other hand we can choose between another kind of clever and interesting programmes such as a Miss World Award or the terrific Scotch Whisky manufacturing story.

Please sir, I would be very grateful if you take out this horrible productions from our little image cages we have in front of the sofa.

Your's faithfully.

---

1 How cohesive is it?
2 How coherent is it?

2 Work in pairs. Decide how you could help the learner to improve the text in activity E1.

REFLECTION

Read the text that you started (and which your classmates continued) in section A again and answer the questions.

a According to the principles you have been looking at in this session, in what ways is the text *cohesive*?
b In what ways is it *coherent*?
c What kind of text (or *text type*) does it belong to (if any)?

40 Professional development and finding a job

A Warm-up

Tick the three things that will most influence you in looking for a teaching job.

- ☐ Earning lots of money
- ☐ Staying near family and friends
- ☐ Travelling
- ☐ Learning about a new culture and a new language
- ☐ Working in a school with a good reputation
- ☐ Gaining any kind of teaching experience

Now walk around the room and find someone who has chosen the same three things.

B Applying for a job

1 Choose a job advertisement. What aspects of your qualifications or experience would you need to highlight in applying for it? Compare ideas with a partner.

University in northern China seeks
EFL qualified
English speaking graduate
to work as an EFL and EAP tutor. Accommodation provided and good local salary. Interviews in London mid-July.

Please send CV to Language Appointments, China, PO Box 4839, quoting reference 53712.

Teaching opportunities in Brazil

We run three schools in São Paulo and require teachers for January start. All ages and levels. Willingness to teach exam classes, particularly FCE, essential.
**For more information contact
a.senna@spschools.br**

Qualified
ELT teachers

required.

Language Partners recruits for schools around Europe. We require both experienced teachers (Cambridge Delta, or equivalent) for DoS positions, and have opportunities for new teachers. (Cambridge Celta or equivalent).

Please send cv to Jenna James, Language Partners, 207 Academy Terrace, London, W3, UK, stating preferred destinations.

Local language knowledge preferred. Visit our website for more information: www.languagepartners.co.uk

2 Work in groups. Make a list of questions you could ask at an interview that would be appropriate for almost any teaching context. Then compare your list with another group's. Here are some possible topics:

- learners
- teachers
- syllabus
- materials and resources
- working conditions

C Professional development

1   Rate the following parts of the CELTA course in terms of their impact on your learning. Compare ideas with a partner.

Course element	Very strong impact	Not so strong impact
input sessions		
planning teaching practice lessons		
teaching		
post-teaching feedback		
writing evaluations of your own lessons		
researching and writing course assignments		
experiencing the foreign language lesson		
tutorials with tutors		
course reading, e.g. handouts, articles, chapters from books		
observation of colleagues		
observation of practising teachers		
informal talk with colleagues		
other (what, exactly?)		

2   Work in groups. In the light of the above, discuss ways to continue developing as a teacher after the course.

D Learning from experience

The learning principle that underpins the CELTA course is, essentially, one of 'reflecting on experience'. That is, learning takes place through cycles of action and reflection.

1   Study the reflective learning cycle and say how it reflects the way the CELTA course was designed and run.

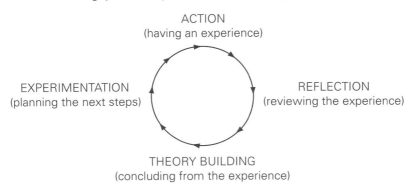

ACTION
(having an experience)

EXPERIMENTATION
(planning the next steps)

REFLECTION
(reviewing the experience)

THEORY BUILDING
(concluding from the experience)

2   Work in pairs. Discuss how the learning cycle will continue in the future. What can you do to keep it 'well oiled' and in good working condition? For example, how can you build a *reflection* stage into your teaching experience?

D Professional development

Research suggests that different people are disposed to different orientations on the learning cycle. We can characterise these dispositions in this way:

the activist:	'I'll try anything once.'
the reflector:	'I'd like time to think about it.'
the theorist:	'What's the theory behind it?'
the pragmatist:	'How can I apply this in practice?'

(adapted from *The Manual of Learning Styles*
Honey and Mumford)

In terms of your future teacher development, your learning style will influence the way you respond to different learning opportunities. For example, an activist would probably respond positively to this situation:

Your school has been asked by a leading ELT publisher to pilot some new teaching materials that they are trialling. They are looking for volunteers to try out the materials in their classes …

However, the activist may feel less enthusiastic about this aspect of the deal:

… Teachers will be asked to complete a questionnaire and write a short report on their experience using the materials.

3 Read the text above and decide which of the following teacher development activities would suit an activist, a reflector, a theorist, and a pragmatist:

a keeping a teaching journal, or web-log (blog)
b learning a foreign language
c reading and discussing articles about language learning
d asking learners to complete feedback questionnaires
e observing other teachers
f team-teaching
g collaborative planning and materials production
h attending conferences
i being observed by a director of studies
j conducting a small-scale research study
k joining an on-line discussion group that focuses on a particular aspect of teaching
l taking special responsibility for an aspect of the school's teaching programme

4 Which of the above activities would suit *you*? What does this say about your preferred learning style?

E Practical steps

Work in pairs or groups. Prepare some questions about any of the following topics. How can you find out the answers?

- professional teaching organisations
- professional newspapers, journals, etc.
- websites, discussion groups
- books about teaching/language
- Diploma/MA courses

REFLECTION

Draw up an 'action plan' for your first six months of teaching. Then work in groups and compare your plans.

Teaching practice

Teaching practice (often called TP) is a core component of the course and the one that gives the course its essentially practical nature. By giving you the opportunity to teach classes of real learners, TP prepares you for the reality of the classroom, and provides a means for putting into practice the techniques and procedures that are discussed in the input sessions. And, TP provides an ongoing cycle of planning, teaching, and reflection, and thereby provides an experientially driven model for your future professional development.

TP is timetabled continuously throughout the course. Each centre will organise TP differently, but it will always involve each trainee teaching at least two different groups (at a minimum of two different levels). Lessons may vary in length, but in all centres the total amount of supervised teaching will add up to six hours for each candidate. After the lesson, the trainer will conduct a feedback session, normally involving other trainees.

1   Ask your trainer about the way TP is organised in your centre.

To get the maximum benefit from TP, and to ease some of the anxieties associated with it, you may find the following advice helpful.

Planning

Go easy!

You will usually be given a section of a coursebook, or a specific language item (often called a 'TP point'), to teach. Stick to this – don't try and teach everything you know about English! If you're asked to teach six items of vocabulary, don't attempt more than six. If you're asked to teach one specific use of a grammar structure, don't attempt to teach all its other uses as well. If you're asked to teach one page of a unit of a coursebook, don't teach the whole unit.

Liaise

It's often the case that you will be sharing the lesson with your colleagues, each taking their turn in the overall sequence. This usually means that you will be working from the same material. It is imperative, therefore, that you are each clear as to which sections of the material you are doing, so that there is no obvious doubling up. You will also need to check which parts of the lesson sequence are dependent on what has gone before. For example, is the person who follows on from you depending on your having taught some key vocabulary?

Research

Do some research into the language area you are going to teach. Consult a grammar reference book (there are some listed in the Reference section) or look at the grammar reference section of your coursebook. At the same time, don't simply regurgitate the contents of the grammar reference in your lesson plan. Your job is to make the teaching point accessible and memorable for the learners.

Manage your time

Try not to spend much longer planning the lesson than would be reasonable in real working conditions. In other words, don't stay up all night planning a twenty-minute lesson.

Be economical

Don't try and re-invent the wheel. If you have been asked to teach some coursebook material, you don't have to rewrite it or redesign it. Remember that it is your *teaching* skills that are being developed, not your ability as a materials writer or graphic artist.

Be flexible

Don't overplan – allow for the unexpected, e.g. a late start, or a new learner, or a problem you hadn't foreseen, and keep your plan flexible. Don't try and put more than is realistically achievable into your lesson. At the same time, it's also a good idea to have one extra activity 'up your sleeve', just in case you have time to spare.

Structure your lesson

Plan around a basic lesson format that makes sense to you and that will make sense to the learners, such as one that has a beginning, a middle and an end. For example, the beginning might be a short ice-breaker, the middle might be the presentation of a grammar structure, and the end might be personalised practice.

Prioritise

Decide what the main activity of the lesson should be: reading, or speaking, for example, or writing, or listening. This will often be specified in the TP point. Make sure your plan foregrounds this core activity, and that it is not pushed to the end of the lesson by lots of preparatory stages.

Build in variety

At the planning stage, think how you will vary the focus of the lesson – so that some of the focus is on you, some is on the learners, and some is on a reading text or listening passage, for example. Even in a twenty- or thirty-minute lesson it's possible to have three different activities, and three different types of interaction.

Be resourceful

Don't overburden yourself with materials, such as photocopies, or with technological aids, such as the overhead projector – unless you feel that they add real value to the lesson. The more 'stuff' you bring into the classroom, the more chance you will lose your way, or things will go wrong. Also, the more you attempt to 'plug every hole' in the lesson, the fewer opportunities there will be for spontaneity and learner participation.

2 Ask your trainer about lesson planning at your centre.

Teaching

Be prepared

Make sure you have everything that you need with you. If you have prepared a worksheet, make sure you have sufficient copies. If you are playing audio material, make sure it is set up to play at the right place. At the very least you will need a board pen. Remember that it doesn't create a good impression if you have to leave the room for something you have forgotten.

Learn their names

Learn and use the learners' names. This is a common courtesy; it also makes classroom management a lot easier.

Don't overrun

You only have a limited amount of time to teach your lesson, and you are likely to be sharing the same class with your colleagues, so it is imperative that you start and finish on time. If you are worried that you may run over time, organise with a colleague, or your trainer, some means by which they signal that you have, say, only five minutes left.

Start on time

The class starts when there are learners in the room – even if only just one. But don't launch into your prepared lesson when the bulk of the class still haven't arrived. Spend this time chatting, or reviewing the last lesson, or checking homework. Good lines to achieve this include: *How was your day? Did you have a good weekend? What are you doing after the lesson / tonight / at the weekend?* And ask the learner(s) to ask you the same or similar questions. If there are two learners, they can ask and answer these questions in a pair.

Focus on the learners

Focus your attention on the learners throughout your lesson, and not on your supervisor or your colleagues. Witty asides to your colleagues are likely to be misinterpreted by the learners.

Look calm

You are likely to feel nervous, but you don't need to *look* nervous. Try and find a 'still point' in the classroom and stay there: it may be seated, or standing. Try and maintain a natural speaking voice, as if you were not really in a classroom at all. Exploit opportunities for laughter – this helps defuse the tension.

Don't panic!

If you lose your way in the lesson, and are not sure what to do next, don't panic. Stop and consult your plan: the learners know that this is an experimental situation, so they are not expecting a totally fluid, professional lesson.

Adapt

Even if you think you are running out of time, don't rush. It may be better to skip a stage, if it means getting to your main activity. Be prepared to abandon or adapt parts of your planned lesson if you feel that these parts are simply not working as planned. Remember that during the feedback on the lesson you will have a chance to talk through your 'in-flight' decisions.

Observe

When you are not teaching but are observing the lessons of your colleagues, give them your full attention. This is not just a question of courtesy: you will probably be asked to comment on your colleagues' lessons during the feedback session. Also, you can learn a lot about the learners by observing the way they respond to different techniques and teaching styles. But avoid becoming involved in the lesson in any way – for example, by answering questions that learners may try to address to you. Indicate to the learners that they should ask the teacher who is currently teaching them.

Teaching practice

3   Ask your trainer about how TP is conducted at your centre.

Finally, here are some common criticisms that have been collected from trainers' assessments of TP lessons.

4   Work in pairs. Choose one or two of the following criticisms. Discuss how you could avoid them.

- You directed your attention at one half of the class only.
- You added 'OK?' to virtually everything you said.
- You wrote everything on the board in capital letters.
- You allowed one or two learners to dominate.
- You were talking to the learners while you were writing on the board with your back to them.
- After each new word that you presented, you asked 'Do you understand?'
- You didn't give time for learners to answer your questions.
- You kept a sort of running commentary on what you were doing, or going to do, throughout the lesson.
- You started giving the instructions for the activity before you had got their full attention.
- Everything that the learners said you wrote onto the board, in a rather random way.
- During the pairwork stage, you spent a lot of time helping one learner, without noticing that the other learners had finished and were chatting in Portuguese.
- You adopted a rather unnatural delivery, as if you were speaking to a child, or someone hard of hearing.
- You set up the groupwork task nicely, but you didn't go round the groups and check that they were doing it properly.
- While the learners were reading the text, you kept distracting them by giving extra instructions.

5   Read these more positive comments. Which ones do you hope will be applied to you? Compare ideas with a partner.

- You were very centred, and you were able to draw the learners' attention.
- You used a natural but intelligible speaking style.
- I liked the way you made sure all the learners had a chance to participate.
- I was impressed by the fact that you used the learners' names throughout.
- It was a good idea, demonstrating the task with one of the learners, before they went into pairs.
- I liked the way you encouraged the learners to expand on their contributions, from single words and phrases to fuller utterances.
- You responded naturally to what the learners said, before correcting the way that they were saying it.
- When you realised that the learners were confused, you stopped the task and gave them clear instructions.
- The boardwork was legible and well organised.
- I liked the way you provided individual help to learners when they needed it, while keeping an eye on the rest of the class.
- It was good that you gave the instructions for the task before putting the learners into their groups.
- Your wrap-up at the end was a nice way to close the lesson.

Post-teaching

Accentuate the positive

Few if any lessons go as planned, so don't punish yourself if you feel that yours didn't. Even if you weren't satisfied with the lesson, think of it as a learning process. Try to identify the strengths of the lesson, not only its weaknesses. The important thing is that you can extract some action points from the lesson that you will be able to apply in the future.

Take responsibility

At the same time, don't disclaim responsibility for the lesson by, for example, blaming the learners, or the coursebook, or the TP point. Effective teachers adapt to the constraints that are imposed on them.

Reflect

After the lesson, take some time to reflect on the lesson. Below there are some ways of framing the reflecting process, in the form of reflection tasks. (Your trainer may assign one of these tasks as the basis for the post-lesson feedback session.) Or you may like to come back to them when you start your first job. In any case, you do not need to use all of them – choose formats with which you are most comfortable.

Keep a journal

You may be asked to keep a training journal – that is, a private written log of your experience learning to become a teacher. You can use any of the reflection tasks to structure your journal; there are some special journal tasks as well.

Reflection tasks

Reflection task 1

Think about your lesson and answer the questions.

- What happened according to plan?
- What *didn't* happen according to plan?
- What happened that I didn't expect?
- What would I do differently next time, and why?

Reflection task 2

Complete the sentences.

- My main aim in this lesson was …
- I achieved my main aim partially/completely.
- As evidence I would mention …

Or:

- I didn't achieve my main aim because …
- My subsidiary aim(s) was/were …
- I achieved my subsidiary aims partially/completely.
- As evidence I would mention …

Or:

- I didn't achieve my subsidiary aims because …

Teaching practice

Reflection task 3

Complete these sentences in as many ways as you can:

- I was happy with the way …
- I wasn't so happy with the way …
- Next time, I'd ….

Reflection task 4

Mark your evaluation of the lesson on these clines (0 = totally disagree; 5 = totally agree)

Statement	Evaluation
1 I achieved what I was aiming to do.	0 1 2 3 4 5
2 I managed the class effectively.	0 1 2 3 4 5
3 I involved all the learners.	0 1 2 3 4 5
4 I used the time effectively.	0 1 2 3 4 5
5 I used the materials/aids effectively.	0 1 2 3 4 5

Reflection task 5

Before the lesson, write down two or three personal objectives you hope to achieve.

After the lesson, evaluate the extent to which you achieved them.

Write some more objectives for your next lesson.

Reflection task 6

What did you learn from this lesson? Summarise what you learned in the form of statements.

- I learned that …
- I learned that …
- I learned that …

What are you still unsure about? Summarise your uncertainties in the form of questions. For example:

- Why …?
- When …?
- How …?
- How much …?
- …

Reflection task 7

Write a report on your lesson. Complete the table.

Subject*	Grade (A – D)	Comments
Planning		
Classroom management		
Use of resources/aids		
Manner and rapport		
Dealing with language issues		
Dealing with error		
Dealing with individuals		
Achievement of aims		
Summary		

* You can add extra 'subjects' if you wish.

Reflection task 8

Work in groups. Design a short feedback questionnaire for the learners to complete in the last few minutes of each lesson. The object of the questionnaire is to give you feedback on the effectiveness of the lessons – but it is *not* to compare teachers. Typical questions might be:

- What was the most important or most interesting thing you learned in this lesson?
- What activity would you like to do again?
- What activity would you *not* like to do again?
- Was there anything missing from the lesson?

Alternatively, provide sentence stems for the learners to complete:

- I learned …
- I enjoyed it when ….
- I didn't like it so much when …
- I would like to do more ….
- I don't really want to do more …

Collect the feedback forms from the learners at the end of the lesson and compare their responses with your own evaluation of the lesson.

Journal tasks

Journal task 1: narrative

Write a narrative account of the lesson, saying what happened.

- Compare this to your plan.
- Explain any departures from the plan.
- Draw some conclusions from this experience.

Teaching practice

Journal task 2: key event

Focus on a 'key event' in the lesson, that is – a significant moment that stands out in your recall of the lesson.

- Why was this event significant?
- What did you learn from it?

Journal task 3: focus on a learner

Choose one learner to focus on, and keep a journal record of his or her progress over a number of lessons.

- Record your own assessment and those of your colleagues.
- You should do this task with the consent of the learner concerned. You can then ask the learner to read your account and to make their own comments. This will allow you to judge, for example, to what extent your inferences were correct.

Journal task 4: recording the lesson

Audio- or video-record a segment of your lesson (you can ask a colleague to do the recording).

Play it back, and transcribe a section of it.

Analyse this section with a view to answering questions such as:

- How natural is my classroom language?
- How intelligible am I? How clear are my instructions?
- Do I have any obtrusive mannerisms (either vocal or gestural)?
- How naturally do I interact with the learners?

Journal task 5: feedback and reflection

Record your reflections on the lesson.

Record your reflections on the feedback that you were given – by your trainer, by your colleagues, or by the learners themselves.

- How useful was the feedback?
- Was it fair? Was it balanced?
- Did the feedback match your own assessment of the lesson?
- How do you think you will take the feedback into account in planning and teaching future lessons?
- What have you learned about *giving* feedback?

Journal task 6: self-evaluation

At periodic points in your journal – such as at the end of each week if you are on a full-time course – answer these questions[1]:

- How am I developing as a language teacher?
- What are my strengths? What are my limitations at present?
- How can I improve my teaching?
- How am I helping my learners?
- What satisfaction does language teaching give me?

1 adapted from Richards, J. and Ho, B. Reflective thinking through Journal Writing. In Richards, J. (1998) *Beyond Training*, CUP, p. 170.

Classroom observation

These observation tasks are for use when observing the teaching practice lessons of your colleagues or any other classes that you are required to observe during the course. Each task has a particular focus, and links to some aspect of the course input. Some tasks focus on the teacher, others focus on the learners, and some focus on the interaction between both teacher and learners. These tasks are designed to provide a focus for post-observation discussion. Normally, your trainer will tell you which task you should use. (Note that there is no obligation to complete all the tasks.)

Observation task 1: the teacher's position and body language

Note the teacher's/teachers' position and movement. If possible, draw a ground plan showing the teacher's movements during the lesson.

- When and where do they sit?
- When and where do they stand?
- How near do they approach the learners at different parts of the lesson?
- When do they move around?
- Do they project to all the learners?
- Can they be heard and seen clearly by all the learners?
- Do they use gesture effectively?
- Do they make eye contact with individual learners?

Observation task 2: the individual learners

Make sure you know the learners' names! Observe the learners and complete the table with their names.

Name	Behaviour
	takes the initiative, volunteers answers to questions, and asks questions of his/her own
	avoids answering questions, or only answers if called on by name; doesn't participate much in open class
	takes part actively in pairwork and groupwork
	tends to take a back-seat role in group work, and does only the minimum in pairwork
	takes risks with the language, and isn't afraid of making mistakes
	is hesitant, even reluctant, to speak
	catches on quickly and follows explanations relatively easily
	often gets confused and frequently seeks clarification from peers

Classroom observation

Observation task 3: interaction

Observe the different *interactions* in each lesson and complete the table. Then answer the questions.

- What is the predominant type of interaction?
- Does it seem appropriate to the aims of the lesson?
- In which interaction were the learners most productive?

Interaction pattern	Amount of time spent
Teacher – whole class	%
Learners in pairs	%
Learners in groups	%
Learners working individually	%
Other	%

Observation task 4: meaning

- Are there any points during the lessons when the learners seem unclear as to what something *means*? How can you tell?
- How is the problem resolved?
- Does the teacher deliberately seek to *check understanding*?
- How is this done?
- How effective is it?

Observation task 5: instructions

- Are there any points in the lesson when learners seem unsure of what the teacher wants them to do? Why is this, do you think?
- Write down, word for word, some examples of instructions that occur during the lesson(s). Are they clear, economical and effective?

Observation task 6: engagement/interest

To what extent do the learners seem *engaged* by the lesson? What is the level of learner *interest*? Plot their engagement over the course of the lesson using this graph (100% = maximally engaged; 0% = totally uninterested):

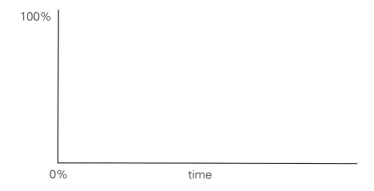

Note: You could do this task to record your impression of the group as a whole or of an individual learner.

Observation task 7: learner participation

Choose *one* learner to focus on (preferably one that you can see and/or hear well) and answer the questions.

- How much speaking (in English!) does he or she do during the lesson?
- How many contributions does he or she make in the whole class stages (as opposed to in pair- or groupwork)?
- Do these contributions take the form of one- or two-word utterances, or complete sentences?
- At any point does the learner contribute more than a sentence?

Observation task 8: teacher–learner interaction

Draw a 'map' of the class, like the one below, and label each learner. Draw lines and arrows to indicate the different interactions between the teacher and individuals, or between individuals and the teacher. The direction of the arrow should indicate whether the interaction is teacher-initiated or learner-initiated. Then answer the questions.

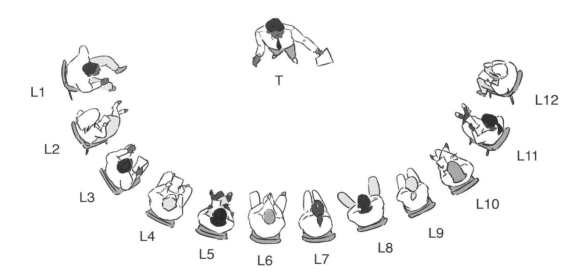

- What does your interaction map suggest?
- What is the dominant direction of interaction?
- With which learners did the teacher interact most?
- Which learners initiated most?

Classroom observation

Observation task 9: error and correction

Note down any instances of learner error, the teacher's response (if any) and the learner's response, e.g. self-correction.

Learner's error	Teacher's response	Learner's response

Observation task 10: planning and staging

Observe a lesson without knowing in advance how it was planned. As you observe the lesson, note the main stages.

- Is there a clear division into stages? For example, is there a beginning, middle and end?
- How is each new stage signalled?
- What is the aim of each stage?
- If possible, after the lesson compare your impression of the lesson's design with the teacher's plan. What differences were there?

Observation task 11: boardwork

Note down at what points in the lesson the teacher uses the board.

- Are there clearly differentiated boardwork stages, or is the board used intermittently throughout the lesson?
- What is written on the board? And where? How legible is it?
- Do the learners copy what is written on the board?
- If possible, ask to look at a learner's book at the end of the lesson, and see if the learner's record of the lesson is an accurate summary of the lesson. To what extent is the learner's record of the lesson a reflection of the boardwork?

Observation task 12: time-on-task

Draw a pie-chart to show the proportion of time-on-task.

- How much time is spent leading up to tasks (including pre-teaching, giving instructions, etc.)?
- How much time do the learners spend engaged on the tasks?
- How much time is spent on the post-task phase (e.g. checking, reporting back, etc.)?

Observation task 13: mother tongue use

Record the *L1 quotient* during the lesson on a graph (100% = all the learners are speaking their L1 all the time; 0% = all the learners are speaking English all the time). Then answer the questions.

* How much use do the learners make of their first language?
* How do you account for any peaks in the graph?
* Would you judge the use of the L1 to be largely constructive or largely unhelpful?

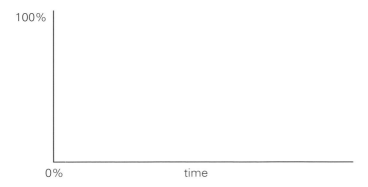

Observation task 14: teacher questions

Monitor the teacher's questioning techniques, and answer the questions.

* How many *real questions* does the teacher ask? (These are questions for which the teacher doesn't know the answer, such as *What did you do at the weekend?*)
* How many display questions does the teacher ask? (These are questions the teacher asks in order for learners to display their knowledge, such as *What is the past of the verb 'go'?*)
* What is different about the stages in the lesson when there is a high proportion of real questions, as opposed to stages which are dominated by display questions?

Real questions	Display questions

Observation task 15: teachers' 'in-flight' decisions

Observe a lesson for which there is a detailed lesson plan. Keep a record of how closely the lesson follows the plan and answer the questions.

a Are there any points when the actual lesson departs from the plan?
b Does the actual timing differ from the anticipated timing of the lesson?
c Can you account for these differences?
d If possible, talk to the teacher after the lesson. How does your account of the teacher's 'in-flight' decisions compare with his/her own?

Classroom observation

Observation task 16: pronunciation

Keep a note of any pronunciation errors that occur in the lesson. Answer the questions and complete the table.

- What effect does the error have on communication?
- Does the error cause a misunderstanding or breakdown in communication and, if so, between whom?
- What is the outcome, e.g. is the error corrected by the teacher, self-corrected by the learner, or ignored?

Error	Should have been	Effect on communication	Outcome
....	....	....	....
....	....	....	....
....	....	....	....

Observation task 17: coursebook use

Observe a lesson that is based on coursebook material. Monitor how closely the lesson follows the coursebook. Use the following cline to record the extent to which the lesson follows the coursebook. (100% = the lesson follows the coursebook exactly; 0% = the lesson bears no resemblance to the coursebook material).

100% ———————————————————————————————— 0%

If possible, compare your evaluation with the teacher's own assessment of how closely the lesson followed the coursebook. What was the effect of either following the coursebook closely, or not following it closely?

Observation task 18: use of technology/aids

Observe a lesson in which the teacher is using some form of technology or aid and answer the questions.

- What technology or aid is the teacher using, e.g. cassette recorder, video, overhead projector or interactive whiteboard?
- How 'fluent' is the teacher with the use of this aid?
- Does it contribute to the flow of the lesson, or does it disrupt it?
- To what extent does the technological aid enhance the lesson?
- Could the lesson aims have been achieved as effectively without it?

Observation task 19: teacher talking time

Make a pie chart to show how much time the teacher talks, and how much time the learners talk.

- Who spends more time talking, the teacher or the learners?
- At what points in the lesson do the learners talk more?
- At what points in the lesson does the teacher talk more?
- Approximately how much of the learner talking time is spent talking in open class?
- Approximately how much of the learner talking time is spent talking in pairs or small groups?
- Does the teacher ever address small groups or individuals 'privately' (i.e. without the whole class hearing)?

Observation task 20: you choose!

Decide what aspect of your class you would like your colleagues to observe.

While watching my lesson, I would like you to monitor / observe / note down any instance of the following:

1.
2.
3.

Tutorials and assignments

Tutorials

During your course you will have the opportunity to speak to your tutor on a one-to-one basis. Your tutor will keep a written record of your tutorial, which you will need to sign. You will have the opportunity to discuss how you feel about the course generally and specifically you will talk about your progress with the written assignments and your teaching practice. The tutorials will be based around the 'progress records' in your CELTA 5 booklet.

The number of tutorials you have is not fixed, but remember that your tutors will be happy to discuss your progress with you and so you can ask to make additional appointments, if you feel you need to.

Before your tutorial

Look at the list of criteria in the CELTA booklet. If you do not understand any of them, then look in the back of the booklet, where they are explained. If you are still unsure, ask your tutor to explain them.

For each criterion you should consider whether you feel you are meeting the necessary standard. Try to think of examples from your teaching practice and also think back to the feedback you have received.

During your tutorial

Remember, your tutorials are two-way processes – you need to speak and also listen to your tutor. Try to be as honest and open as you can be. If there is anything that you do not understand, do not be afraid to say so.

Your tutorial will be based around the list of points in your CELTA booklet, although your tutor may not comment on all of them in detail, as time may be limited.

If you need to, make a note of any important points that you wish to raise before the tutorial and take it in with you, so that you do not forget what you want to say.

After your tutorial

Think carefully about what was said. Read the notes that your tutor made and, if you agree with the summary, sign the page in the CELTA booklet.

Ensure you understand the points you need to work on and also how to make progress in these areas. If you are not sure, you could read relevant books on the topic, look back at notes you have made during input sessions, or ask your tutor for further guidance. When you next teach, try to include evidence of having worked on relevant points in the way you plan the lesson, the way you teach it and also when you reflect on the lesson in feedback.

Written assignments

There are four written assignments on the CELTA course. They are:

* Focus on the learner
* Language-related tasks
* Skills assignment
* Lessons from the classroom

In total you should write around 3000 words and your centre will give you guidance on how much to write for each assignment. The centre will also give you the criteria by which your work will be assessed. It is very important that you read and understand these before you start writing. The precise wordings of the assignments will vary from centre to centre, but these criteria are standardised and are the same in all centres.

The work you submit must be your own. If you include quotes or take ideas from other sources, you must acknowledge where these come from.

If your first submission of an assignment is not up to the required standard, you are allowed to resubmit it one more time. If necessary, you can resubmit all four assignments. Your grade is not affected by resubmitting work. In order to pass the written component of the course, and therefore the course overall, you must pass three out of the four assignments.

A proportion of all the assignments will be 'double-marked' – that is to say, two tutors will read the assignment and agree marks. This is a way of standardising the process and ensuring that it is fair.

For each assignment you should also read the instructions very carefully so that you know exactly what you are expected to write. If you are not sure, then ask for further clarification.

Things to remember

Writing can be viewed as a process – there are stages you go through before ending up with the final 'product'. You may find it helpful to clearly distinguish the stages in your mind – research, planning, producing a draft, editing the work, redrafting, checking for spelling and grammar mistakes and so on.

Think of who you are writing for. Your tutor will read the work, but so too may an external assessor. It is important that the tone is not too informal – it should either be in a slightly academic style, or be neutral.

Using headings and sub-headings can help the reader to follow your arguments and are appropriate in most assignments.

Things that can go wrong

Time management

Your centre will tell you when you should hand work in. It is important that you make every effort to meet the deadlines set because otherwise you may find work piling up towards the end of the course.

Fulfilling requirements

It is very important that you actually do what you are asked to do in the assignment. When you have drafted your assignment, check the wording of the task to ensure that you have included all the components required.

Tutorials and assignments

Relevance

Although 3000 words may sound a lot, that is for all four assignments. You will probably find it a challenge to include all you want to say in the number of words you have for each assignment. It is therefore important that you write concisely and include only relevant information.

Look at the following extract from the *Focus on the learner* assignment. Is there any information which is not necessary?

> Cinzia lives in a small town in the north of Italy, Saronno. Saronno is famous for the production of a drink called 'Amaretto', although Cinzia herself is not keen on it. Cinzia is a doctor and she combines a busy professional life with bringing up her two children (Eugenia, 9, and Carlo, 7). She learned a little English at school but says she was easily bored and preferred maths and science subjects. As a doctor she needs to be able to read medical journals, which are often published in English, and one of her motivations for learning English is to allow her to do this. She also attends conferences and would like to develop some 'social conversation skills'. When not working or studying, Cinzia likes to watch her favourite football team, AC Milan, and she tries to attend at least three or four matches a season.

Detail

Although it is important to only include relevant information, you also need to include detail where necessary. In the *Focus on the learner* assignment, for example, you may well be asked to include a reference to specific material to help the learner with an identified difficulty. Compare these two responses:

> Jurgen wishes to improve his grammar, so something from Oxford Practice Grammar Intermediate (Eastwood, OUP) would be appropriate.

> Jurgen wishes to improve his grammar. I noticed in my conversations with him that he made several errors using reported speech (see transcript on page 7) and so I would recommend *Oxford Practice Grammar Intermediate* (Eastwood, OUP) section 132 (page 318) which deals with this and provides practice that he could do outside class time.

Accuracy of information

It is important that what you write is accurate. Here is part of a *Language-related tasks* assignment:

> **Analyse the form and meaning of the underlined parts of the sentences. Suggest a context in which the sentence could be introduced. In each case say how you would check understanding. You do not need to write in complete sentences.**
>
> **1** <u>Would you like</u> an ice cream?
> **2** <u>Are you going</u> on holiday next week?

Now look at a trainee's response. Consider the accuracy and detail of the work and then grade it as 'Good', 'Average' or 'Below standard'.

1   *Would you like an ice cream?*
    Would + subject + verb
    Used to make offers.
    Context: parent to a child
    Checking: I'd ask questions.
2   *Are you going on holiday next week?*
    going to future
    talking about the future
    Context: in a pub
    Checking: I'd ask questions

Now look at another trainee's response. Again, grade the work as 'Good', 'Average' or 'Below standard', according to the accuracy and detail.

1   *Would you like an ice cream?*
    would + subject + base form of the verb
    Used to make an offer
    Context: parent to a child, standing by an ice-cream van on a hot day. I might introduce this with a picture in a lesson. Clearly the child should not be holding an ice-cream.
    Checking: I'd ask a question such as:
    'Is this about one time, now, or something that the child always likes?' (one time)

2   *Are you going on holiday next week?*
    'present continuous' (question form *be* + *subject* + *present participle*)
    Used to talk about future plans/arrangements
    Context: two colleagues talking
    Checking: I'd ask questions such as:
    'Has he already planned the holiday?'
    'Do you think he has bought his plane ticket already?'

Tutorials and assignments

Standard of written English

As a teacher you will have to teach writing skills. It is therefore important that you demonstrate your ability to write accurately in terms of spelling, grammar and linking.

Look at the following piece of writing taken from the *Lessons from the classroom* assignment. Do you think it is of an appropriate standard for a teacher of English?

> When I start teaching I knew that my writting on the board was not great – not at all. The tutor told me in the first lesson that it was a bit iffy but I tried for the next lesson. There's alot of things to learn when you start teaching because there's grammer, vocabulary and skills. I was maybe thinking too much about all of them things to really be able to do myself justice.

Warmers and fillers

Many teachers find it useful to a have a bank of short activities that they can use during lessons. These short activities are often referred to as 'warmers' or 'fillers'. They can be useful to change the pace of the lesson, to help learners relax, to help build the dynamics of the group and to give variety. They are often used at the start of lessons, but they can be exploited at any point in a lesson to help to improve the quality of the activity that follows. Some warmers have a clear linguistic element (such as vocabulary revision) but others focus on relaxing learners, or conversely, on building energy levels in the group. Many can be done either as a whole class activity or in small groups. The teacher needs to assess the appropriacy of these short activities. Some groups enjoy and benefit from them, while other may feel that they are a block to focussing on the main point.

Getting to know you

My name is ... and I like ...

A memory game. Go round the class: the first person completes the formula *My name is ... and I like ...*. The next person reports this (*Her name is ... and she likes ...*) and then adds their own name and something they like, and so on, each person reporting on what everyone else has said, before adding something new.

Five-pointed star

Learners each draw a five-pointed star. On the first point they write a person's name that is important to them; on the second a place name; on the third a number; on the fourth a date; and on the fifth a sign, symbol or logo. They then get into pairs or small groups, show each other their stars, and ask and answer questions about them.

Phonemic likes and dislikes

Write the following questions on the board in phonemic script:
Who's your favourite actor? What kind of music do you like? What was the last book you read?
Learners write their answers in phonemic script. They then show each other – and comment on – their answers.

Maps

The learners imagine the room as a map (establish north, south, east and west, and where one country is on the 'map') – they must then go and stand on the country they would most like to visit and talk to others who are near them about why they have chosen that part of the world.

Last weekend

In pairs learners ask and answer *yes/no* questions in order to find out as much as possible about their partner's weekend. They then report to the class.

In a line

Ask learners to organise themselves into a line according to specific criteria, e.g. birthday, distance they travel to get to the centre, number of foreign countries visited, alphabetical order of given (first) names, etc.

What I like about you is …

Learners work in small groups. One member of the group should remain silent while the other members have 30 seconds to pay as many compliments as they can to that person, beginning *What I like about you is …*.

Back to back

In pairs learner stand back to back and have to then guess what the other is wearing by asking *yes/no* questions: *Are you wearing socks? Are they black?* etc.

Word games

Hangman

One person thinks of a word and represents each letter with a line. Others guess the letters that make up the word. If they guess incorrectly, then another part of the 'hangman picture' is added.

What word?

The teacher gives a word to a learner, who must then represent the word either by drawing a picture or through mime. Others guess the word. This can be played as a team game.

Kim's game

The teacher collects seven or eight possessions from members of the class (with their permission) and then covers them. The learners must remember what items were collected and who they belonged to.

Vocabulary quiz

The teacher prepares a short quiz with questions such as:
Think of five things that are green.
Think of three things that are thinner than a pencil.
Think of six things you could keep money in.

Letters to words

The teacher gives the class a collection of letters, and learners have to form as many words as they can using each letter only once in each word.

Alphabet game

The teacher gives the class (or groups) a topic, e.g. *football* or *cinema*. The learners have to think of a word beginning with each letter of the alphabet that they associate with the topic.

I went to market …

Each learner adds an element to the formula *I went to market and I bought …* and repeats from memory what other learners have said. Variants: *I went to the pharmacy / stationers / clothing department …*; *I packed for a holiday and I packed …*.

Relaxing

Visualisation

Everyone should close their eyes. Play the class a piece of relaxing music. As it plays tell the class a story, or engage them in creating the story by asking questions as they listen.. So, for example, the teacher could say: *You see a beautiful sailing boat on the horizon, with a bright yellow sail,* or *You see a boat on the horizon. What does it look like?*

The learners don't say anything until after the story is finished, when they can share their thoughts.

Our picture

Learners work in pairs and must not talk to each other. They must draw a picture together using one pen, but both of them must be touching the pen at all times.

If I were …

The teacher dictates some *If I were …* sentence stems and the learners complete them and then compare their answers. For example:
If I were a season, I'd be … because …
If I were a colour, I'd be … because …

Classroom quiz

Everyone except one person should close their eyes. That person then asks simple questions about the physical environment, e.g. *How many windows are in the room?*

Paper conversation

Learners work in pairs or small groups, and share one piece of paper. On this they ask and answer questions, as if they were having a conversation, but through writing – not speaking.

Teach a Martian

The teacher poses as an alien and asks the class to tell him/her how to boil an egg. This will involve explaining what an egg is, a chicken, a bird …, etc.

Energy raising

Obsessions

Distribute slips of paper on which different 'obsessions' are written, such as *My baby, The Royal Family, Dieting, Football, Astrology, House prices …*. In small groups, learners have conversations, trying to steer the talk to their own obsession.

Yes/no game

One person must answer *yes/no* questions asked by others but without saying *yes* or *no*.

Finding a partner

The teacher distributes halves of sentences, questions and answers, infinitives and past forms, or anything else where there is a clear 'partner'. The learners mingle and try to find their partner.

My word, your word

Learners work in pairs and must answer questions asked by the rest of the group. However, they are only allowed to say one word at a time, and so must listen to each other to try to form utterances that make sense and are grammatically accurate. For example, question: *What is your favourite time of day?*
A: My
B: favourite
A: time
B: is
and so on.

How do you feel?

Learners must mingle around the room and greet each other, but every few seconds the teacher 'changes their mood' by giving instructions such as: *Say it as if you are exhausted, Say it as if you have just received some really good news, Say it as if you are speaking to a former boyfriend/girlfriend,* etc.

Physical exercise

The teacher gives instructions to the class to do a (very light) physical workout.

Mini-conversation

Learners have a conversation in pairs, but each utterance can only be a maximum of two words long, said with the appropriate intonation. For example:
A: Last night?
B: TV
A: Interesting?
B: Boring …

Who am I?

Attach post-it notes with the names of famous people to learners' foreheads, so they can't see whose name it is. They all circulate, asking and answering questions, e.g. *Am I a film star? Am I American?,* until they have guessed who they are.

Last lesson

Learners write three things that are true about the last lesson and two that are untrue. They then read them out and others have to say whether they are true or not. For example, *Alejandra was speaking Spanish when the teacher came in.*

Brief guide to the English verb

Present simple

Examples

He usually drives to work.
The sun rises in the east.
I don't eat meat.
What time does your train leave?

Uses

* to talk about routines and habits
* to talk about things that are always true
* to talk about schedules and timetables

Form

affirmative base form of the verb (+ -*s* in the third person)
negative subject + *do/does* + *not* + base form
question *do/does* + subject + base form

Past simple

Examples

He played for England in the 1970s.
We didn't see them.
When did you wake up?

Use

* to talk about completed actions in the past

Form

affirmative base form + -*ed* (for regular verbs)
negative subject + *did* + *not* + base form
question *did* + subject + base form

Future with *will*

Examples

You won't win the lottery.
We'll drop by later.
The President will meet the PM on Tuesday.

Uses

* to make predictions about the future
* to express decisions made at the time of speaking
* to give facts about the future

Form

affirmative *will* + base form of the verb
negative subject + *will* + *not* + base form of the verb
question *will* + subject + base form of the verb

Future with *going to*

Examples

She's going to look for a new job.
Are you going to see Juliet later?
I think it's going to snow later.

Uses

* to talk about plans
* to make predictions about the future

Form

affirmative *be* + *going to* + base form of the verb
negative subject + *be* + *not* + *going to* + base form of the verb
question *be* + subject + *going to* + base form of the verb

Present continuous

Examples

He's playing upstairs at the moment.
The climate is changing quite quickly.
What time are we meeting?

Uses

* to talk about things happening now, or around now

- to talk about future plans and arrangements
- to talk about changes

Form

affirmative *am/is/are* + present participle
negative subject + *am/is/are* + *not* + present participle
question *am/is/are* + subject + present participle

Past continuous

Examples

They were having dinner at the Mermaid Inn when we saw them.
Where were they going?

Use

- to talk about an action happening before (and perhaps after) another point in time

Form

affirmative *was/were* + present participle
negative subject + *was/were* + *not* + present participle
question *was/were* + subject + present participle

Future continuous

Examples

I'll be working all day tomorrow.
Phone her now – she'll be watching the cricket.
He'll be meeting the PM later today.

Uses

- to talk about things happening around a point of time in the future
- to talk about planned future events
- to make predictions about things happening at the time of speaking

Form

affirmative *will* + *be* + present participle
negative subject + *will* + *be* + *not* + present participle
question *will* + *be* + subject + present participle

Present perfect simple

Examples

Have you seen 'Casablanca'?
They've lived in the same house for years.
I've fed the cats.

Uses

- to talk about an indefinite point in the past
- to talk about something started in the past and continuing to the present
- to talk about a recently completed action

Form

affirmative *have/has* + past participle
negative subject + *have/has* + *not* + past participle
question *have/has* + subject + past participle

Past perfect simple

Examples

She had decided to leave him before we met.
Had you known each other long before you married?

Use

- to sequence two past actions

Form

affirmative *had* + past participle
negative subject + *had* + *not* + past participle
question *had* + subject + past participle

Future perfect simple

Examples

They'll have been married for three years in June.
Some types of frog will have become extinct by 2050.
He'll have arrived by now, I expect.

Uses

- to say how long something will have been in progress by a point in the future
- to say that something will be finished before a particular point in the future

- to make predictions about things happening at the time of speaking

Form

affirmative *will* + *have* + past participle
negative subject + *will* + *not* + *have* + past participle
question *will* + subject + *have* + past participle

Present perfect continuous

Examples

She's been commuting for years.
Have you been working all night?
What have you been doing?

Uses

- to talk about something started in the past and continuing to the present
- to talk about recently completed actions (particularly if there is some evidence)

Form

affirmative *have/has* + *been* + present participle
negative *have/has* + *not* + *been* + present participle
question *have/has* + subject + *been* + present participle

Past perfect continuous

Examples

We had been playing there for ages before anyone complained.
I hadn't been looking to change my job, but this offer was too good to turn down.

Use

- to say how long something had been in progress before another point in the past

Form

affirmative *had* + *been* + present participle
negative *had* + *not* + *been* + present participle
question *had* + subject + *been* + present participle

Future perfect continuous

Examples

By next month, he'll have been running marathons for fourteen years.
How long will we have been dating by October?

Use

- to say how long something will have been in progress up to a point in the future

Form

affirmative *will* + *have* + *been* + present participle
negative *will* + *not* + *have* + *been* + present participle
question *will* + subject + *have* + *been* + present participle

Glossary

accuracy the extent to which a learner's use of a second language conforms to the standard form of that language; it is often contrasted with **fluency**.

achievement test a test that is given at the end of a course to see how much the learners have learned.

acquisition the process of language development in an individual; it is sometimes used to mean the natural process of picking up a language, in contrast to learning, which involves formal instruction.

active (voice) a verb form such as *makes* or *was writing* where the **subject** is the person doing the action, as compared to the **passive** (*is made, was written*).

adjective a word like *old, blue* or *interesting*, that tells you about the qualities of a person or thing or event.

adverb a word like *quickly, well, here* or *then*, which tells you about the circumstances of an event, such as how or where or when it happens.

affirmative (sentence) a sentence that makes a positive statement, as opposed to a negative one.

affix an element that is added either to the beginning of a word (in the case of **prefixes**, such as *un-, anti-, re-*) or to the end of the word (in the case of **suffixes**, such as *-less, -wise, -ly*) and which change the word's meaning or **part of speech**.

aids the tools or equipment that a teacher uses to assist learning, such as **visual aids**, real objects (**realia**) or the **overhead projector** or DVD player.

aim the learning objective of a teaching sequence; a distinction is made between the main or primary aim and secondary or subsidiary aims; aims are defined in terms of linguistic items, such as verb forms, and also in terms of **skills** development; some teachers also identify interpersonal aims for a lesson, that is, aims that target developing a good class dynamic.

antonym a word, such as *old*, which is opposite in meaning to another word, such as *young* or *new*.

appropriacy, appropriateness the use of language that is suitable for its context, e.g. not too formal in an **informal** context.

article either of the **determiners** *the* (definite article) or *a/an* (indefinite article) as in *the banana, a banana;* when nouns are used without an article, the absence of the article is called **zero article**: *it tastes like banana.*

aspect a verb form that expresses the speaker's view of the event described by the verb, such as whether it is in progress or complete. There are two aspects in English **continuous (progressive)** and **perfect**.

assessment collecting information in order to gauge a learner's progress; assessment may be formal, as in **testing**, or informal, as in simply observing learners doing tasks.

audiolingual method a method of language teaching which foregrounded **drilling** and the learning of **dialogues**.

authentic material classroom material that was not originally written or spoken for language teaching purposes, such as newspaper articles or television documentaries.

auxiliary verb grammar words like *do, had, was* that are used with main verbs, like *want, play, get up*, to form tenses, questions and negatives.

bare infinitive the **infinitive** form without *to*, as in *she made me do it.*

base form (of the verb) the form of the verb that is not inflected by the addition of grammatical elements, such *-ing, -ed, -s.*

brainstorming a group task in which learners freely generate ideas or solutions to problems or language items around a theme.

business English the English that is used in business settings and which is the purpose for which many learners learn English.

checking understanding the process of gauging the learners' grasp of a new concept, by asking **concept questions**, for example.

chunk a phrase of two or more words that is stored and used as a single unit, such as *by the way, head over heels, see you later.*

class profile the description of the learners in a class that forms part of a lesson plan.

classroom management the ways the teacher organises and controls the classroom activity, including the learners' interactions and the use of resources.

clause a group of words containing a **verb**, forming the main structures of which sentences are built *[She was sitting in the waiting-room], [reading a newspaper], [when it was announced [that the train [she was waiting for] had been delayed]].*

cloze test a test consisting of a text in which every *n*th word has been replaced by a space.

collocation the way that certain words regularly occur together, such as *good clean fun*, but not *bad dirty fun.*

Common European Framework a project aimed at providing a common basis for language education in Europe, in such areas as **syllabus** design and **assessment**, and consisting of a description of the components of language proficiency at all levels and across a range of skills.

communicative activity a classroom speaking or writing task in which the learners have to interact in order to solve a problem or complete a task.

communicative approaches language teaching methods whose goal is meaningful communication rather than knowledge of language rules, for example.

Community Language Learning (CLL) a **humanistic** approach to language teaching that borrows techniques used in group counselling and where the learners choose what to talk about while the teacher provides the necessary language.

comparative the form of an adjective or adverb that is used to make comparisons: *older, better, more expensive, less often.*

compound noun a noun formed from two or more individual words, such as *bookshop, hair-dryer, washing machine.*

concept questions questions that a teacher asks in order to check the learners' understanding of a new word or grammar structure.

conditional the form of a verb made with *would/should*, e.g. *I would ask someone*; a conditional clause is one that usually starts with *if*, which tells us about possible or hypothetical situations: *If you don't know a word, look it up. I would ask someone, if I were you.*

conjunction a word like *and, but, so* that links two **clauses** or phrases or words.

connected speech the way that speech sounds are produced as part of a continuous sequence, rather than in isolation.

consonant in pronunciation, a sound that is made when the airflow from the lungs is obstructed in some way.

content-based learning (also **content and language integrated learning** or **CLIL**) the teaching, through English, of a subject, such as geography, natural science or history, to learners whose first language is not English.

context either the text that immediately surrounds a language item (also called **co-text**) or the particular situation in which language is used (also called **context of situation**).

continuous (also **progressive**) the **aspect** of the verb that is formed by combining the **auxiliary verb** *be* with the **present participle**: *she is leaving; it was raining.*

contraction the reduction of some elements that results when joining two words such as a **pronoun** (*they, it*) and an **auxiliary verb** (*will, is*): *they'll, it's.*

Resource file

controlled practice (sometimes called **restricted practice**) a stage in the teaching of a language item in which the learners use the item in restricted contexts so as to gain mastery of the form rather than to use the item communicatively; **drilling** is a form of controlled practice.

corpus (pl. **corpora**) a database of texts, stored digitally, that researchers and writers of dictionaries use to investigate language usage.

countable noun a noun like *day*, *child* or *glass* that refers to something that can be counted and so has a plural form: *days, children, glasses*; uncountable nouns, like *water* or *information*, do not normally have plural forms.

coursebook (also called **textbook**) the book that contains the materials used in a language course, often part of a series, each part aimed at one level.

deductive learning an approach to learning where learners are given rules which they then apply in the creation of examples; it contrasts with **inductive learning**.

determiner a word like *the, some, my, many, no*, etc. that belongs to the class of words that can go at the beginning of a **noun phrase**: _the woman in white_; _my many friends_.

dialogue a model conversation in a coursebook or the activity of practising language through interactive speech.

diphthong a **vowel** sound, such as the ones in *boy* and *cow*, that is made when the tongue changes position to produce a sound like two vowels.

direct method a method of language teaching based on the principle that only the target language should be used in class.

discourse any connected piece of speech or writing; the analysis of its connectedness is called discourse analysis.

Dogme ELT an approach to teaching that advocates the use of minimal resources in order to maximise the learners' own contribution to language learning.

drill, drilling a form of **controlled practice** involving oral repetition of words or sentence patterns. Drilling can be **choral**, when the whole class is repeating the item together, or **individual**.

eliciting the teacher's use of questions so as to involve learners and to find out what they already know.

English as an International Language (EIL) the way English is now used by many non-native speakers to communicate with other non-native speakers; also called **English as a Lingua Franca (ELF)**.

English for Special Purposes (also **English for Specific Purposes; ESP**) a general term for the content of courses that are targeted at groups of learners, such as business people or university students, whose particular vocational or academic needs have been identified; ESP contrasts with general English.

error a non-standard language form produced by learners as the result of incomplete or faulty learning; errors are sometimes contrasted with **mistakes**, which are attributed to the pressures of performance and which can be self-corrected.

extensive reading the reading of longer texts, such as stories or novels, in order to gain a general, not detailed, understanding and often for pleasure.

feedback the messages that learners get about their language use or their language learning; positive feedback is information that the learner's language use has been correct; negative feedback indicates that it has been incorrect.

finger-coding, finger-correction the use of the fingers to represent the elements of a word or phrase in order to display its form or to identify an error.

flashcard a card with pictures or words on it, that is used as a prompt in the classroom.

fluency the capacity to be communicative in real-time conditions; often contrasted with **accuracy**.

focus on form a stage in teaching where the learner's attention is directed to the form of a language item, e.g. when the teacher points out the *-ed* ending on regular past tense verbs.

206

function the communicative purpose of a language item, often described in terms of speech acts, such as *offering, apologising, requesting, asking for information.*

functional exponent one of the ways that a **function** is commonly realised; thus, a functional exponent of *offering* is *Would you like …?*

gap fill an exercise that requires learners to complete a sentence or text in which certain items have been removed.

genre any type of spoken or written **discourse** which is used and recognised by members of a particular culture or sub-culture.

gerund the form of the verb ending in *-ing* and which acts like a noun, as in *No parking*; the term *-ing* **form** is now more generally used.

gist a general understanding of a written or spoken text, as opposed to a detailed understanding; a gist task is one that checks or tests this general understanding.

graded reader an extended reading text whose level of language has been controlled so as to be more easily intelligible for learners.

grading (language) the way teachers simplify their classroom language in the interests of intelligibility, especially with beginners and elementary learners.

grammar the process by which language is organised and patterned in order to make meaning and also the description of the rules that govern this process.

grammar–translation method a language teaching method where the emphasis is on learning the rules of the grammar and in which sentences and texts are translated from the learner's language into the target language and vice versa.

group dynamics the relationship between the members of a group (such as a language class) that contributes to its cohesion and helps motivate its individual members.

groupwork a classroom organisation in which learners work in groups of three or more in order to complete a task.

guided discovery a teaching process that encourages learners to work out rules for themselves, with some teacher guidance.

highlighting (form) techniques that draw learners' attention to the forms of second language items, such as using boardwork to show inversion in question forms.

homophone a word that sounds like another word, but is written differently, such as *sea* and *see*. A homograph is spelled the same as another word but pronounced differently, as in *the long and* <u>*windy*</u> *road; a dark and* <u>*windy*</u> *night*. A homonym is the same in both spelling and pronunciation as another word but different in meaning, as in *a cricket* <u>*bat*</u> and *a vampire* <u>*bat*</u>.

humanistic teaching any teaching approach that prioritises human values and asserts the central role of the whole person, including their feelings, in the learning process.

icebreaker an activity that is planned for the start of a lesson or course and is designed to put learners at their ease and to build a good **group dynamic**.

idiom a phrase whose meaning is not literal and is not deducible from its components, as in *hell for leather* (= *very fast*).

imperative the **base form** of the verb when it is used without a subject to give orders or directions: <u>*Turn*</u> left. Don't <u>*say*</u> that.

indirect question a question that is embedded in a statement or another question, as in *I don't know* <u>*what her name is*</u>; *Can you tell me* <u>*when the bank opens*</u>?

inductive learning an approach to learning in which learners are given examples of a structure and they then work out the rules underlying them; it contrasts with **deductive learning**.

infinitive the **base form** of the verb, used with or without *to* (in the latter case it is called the **bare infinitive**), as in <u>*to be*</u> or not <u>*to be*</u>; *you made me* <u>*love*</u> *you*. When the infinitive expresses an intention it is called the infinitive of purpose: *We stopped* <u>*to admire*</u> *the view.*

informal (language) forms of language, including slang, that are typically used between friends or people from the same social group and which mark their equal status.

information gap activity a type of **communicative activity** in which the information that is necessary in order to complete a task is distributed between the two or more learners who are doing the task, so that they must communicate with one another.

-ing form a word ending in -ing, such as *cooking* or *seeing*, which is used: (1) to form verb tenses, where it is also called the **present participle**, as in *I'm cooking*; and (2) like a noun after certain verbs and prepositions, where it is also called a **gerund**, as in *I like cooking. I look forward to seeing you.*

integrated skills the teaching of the skills (of reading, writing, speaking and listening) in conjunction with one another, rather than separately.

interaction the use of language between people; interaction is considered a necessary condition for language **acquisition**.

interlanguage the grammatical system that a learner creates in the course of learning another language.

intonation the meaningful use of either rising or falling pitch in speech.

intransitive verb a verb like *laugh, go, happen* that doesn't take an **object**: *nobody laughed; something happened.*

irregular verb a verb like *go, say* or *write* whose past form and/or **past participle** does not end in -*ed*.

jazz chant a classroom activity in which learners recite in unison a sequence of words or sentences that have a marked and regular **rhythm**, in order to practise features of **connected speech**.

jigsaw technique a type of **communicative activity** in which information is distributed among the members of a group, so that, in order to complete a task, they must share the information.

L1 the learner's first language or mother tongue.

L2 the learner's second (or possibly third or fourth, etc.) language, which, when it is the object of instruction, is also called the target language.

learner autonomy the capacity of the learner to learn independently of teachers, and one of the goals of **learner training**.

learner training techniques that help learners make the most of learning opportunities, such as ways of recording and memorising incidental vocabulary.

learning strategies techniques or behaviours that learners consciously apply in order to improve their learning, such as asking the meaning of unfamiliar words.

learning style the learner's preferred way of learning, influenced by their personality or by their previous learning experience.

lexical approach an approach to language teaching that foregrounds the importance of vocabulary acquisition, including the learning of **chunks**.

lexical set a group of words that are thematically related, such as *windscreen, steering wheel, handbrake, indicator.*

lexis the vocabulary of a language, as opposed to its **grammar**.

literacy the ability to read and write in a language in order to achieve one's functional goals.

metalanguage the language that is used to talk about language, such as grammatical terminology.

milling, mingling a classroom activity in which learners move around the class and interact with one another in turn, as when conducting a survey, for example.

minimal pair a pair of words which differ in meaning when only one sound is changed, such as *bin* and *bean*, or *ban* and *fan*.

mistake a non-standard language form produced by learners as the result of the pressures of performance in real time, rather than because of incomplete or faulty learning (in which case the non-standard form is often called an **error**).

modal verb a verb such as *can, may, should, must,* etc. which is used to express possibility and to make offers, suggestions, commands, etc. Modal verbs function like **auxiliary verbs**, in combination with main verbs, to form questions and negatives.

modelling providing learners with the spoken form of a language item which they can then imitate.

model text a written example of a particular type of text which learners can imitate.

monitoring the process of observing learners doing a **task** in order to check that they are 'on task', to correct errors and to be available for consultation.

motivation the effort that learners put into language learning as a result of their desire or need to learn the language.

multiple-choice questions test items that give candidates a number of possible answers from which they must choose the correct one.

multiple intelligences a theory that argues that human intelligence has many dimensions, such as verbal, musical and interpersonal, as well as logical/mathematical.

native speaker a person who has acquired a language as a child and therefore has an intuitive understanding of its grammar, as contrasted with a non-native speaker, for whom the language is an **L2**.

needs analysis the process of determining the purposes for which a learner is learning a language and for designing a course (typically an **ESP** course) that is appropriate.

nominating indicating which learner is to answer a question by using their name.

notion an area of meaning, like *location, frequency, possibility,* that is sometime used as a basis for organising language syllabuses, especially notional syllabuses.

noun a word like *bus, driver, journey, fare, request,* etc. that can be used after a **determiner** as the **subject** or **object** of a sentence.

noun phrase a word or group of words consisting of at least a **noun** or a **pronoun** and which functions like a noun: *last night; your old car; I; those big red London buses.*

object a **noun phrase** which refers to what or who is affected by the action described by the verb: *I caught <u>the bus</u>. I paid <u>the driver</u>* (= indirect object) *<u>the fare</u>* (= direct object).

objective test a test that can be marked without requiring the test marker's personal judgement, as opposed to a **subjective test**.

one-to-one a teaching situation where there is one teacher and one learner.

overhead projector (ohp) a device that projects an image or text, in the form of a transparency, on to a board or screen.

pace the flow of activities in a lesson and the variations in the speed and intensity of the activities.

pairwork a classroom organisation in which learners work in pairs in order to complete a task.

part of speech any one of the (usually) eight classifications of words according to their function, i.e. **noun**, **verb**, **adjective**, **pronoun**, **adverb**, **determiner**, **preposition** and **conjunction**.

passive (voice) a verb form such as *is made* or *was written* where the **subject** is the person or thing who is affected by the action, as compared to the **active** (*makes, was writing*).

past continuous (or **progressive**) the form of the verb that combines the past of the **auxiliary verb** *be* with the present participle *it was raining; the dogs were barking.*

past participle a verb form that is used to form the **present perfect** and the **passive** *I have <u>worked</u>. The letter was <u>written</u>.* Regular past participles end in *-ed.*

past perfect the form of the verb that combines the past of the **auxiliary verb** *have* and the **past participle**: *the film had started.* The form *had + been +* **present participle** is called the past perfect continuous (or progressive): *it had been raining.*

past simple the form of the verb that takes an *-ed* ending (for **regular verbs**) and typically expresses past meaning: *Dan called. I sent you an e-mail.*

peer correction the correcting of one learner's **error** by another learner.

perfect the **aspect** of the verb that combines the **auxiliary verb** *have* with the **past participle**: *The post has arrived; It had been raining.*

personalisation the classroom use of language to express one's own feelings, experiences and thoughts.

phoneme any one of the distinctive sounds of a particular language; standard British English has 44 phonemes, distributed between 24 **consonants** and 20 **vowels.**

phonemic chart a classroom aid that displays the 44 phonemes of English in the form of **phonemic script.**

phonemic script the conventional way of representing the **phonemes** of a language; in phonemic script the word *phoneme* is written /ˈfəʊniːm/.

phrasal verb a **verb** that is made up of two parts and which often has idiomatic meaning: *I got up at nine. Do you take after your Dad?*

placement test a test that is designed to place learners in the most suitable class for their ability.

portfolio a collection of examples of a learner's achievements that is assembled for the purposes of **assessment.**

possessive adjective a word like *my, your, her, their* that precedes the **noun** and denotes possession *my bike; your turn.*

possessive pronoun a word like *mine, yours, hers, theirs* that stands for a **noun** and denotes possession: *That bike is mine; Whose turn is it? Yours.*

possessive 's' the use of an apostrophe and *s* at the end of a **noun** to indicate ownership: *Claire's knee; the neighbours' cat.*

PPP (presentation, practice, production) a format for the staging of grammar teaching that starts with the presentation of a new grammar item, followed by **controlled practice** and finally by free production.

prefix → **affix**

preposition a word, or group of words, like *in, on, behind, in front of* which often indicates place or time and is always followed by a **noun phrase**: *in the garden, on Sunday, behind the times.*

present continuous (or **progressive**) the form of the verb that combines the **present** of the **auxiliary verb** *be* with the present **participle**: *it is raining; the doors are opening.*

present participle an **-ing word** that is used to express verbal meaning: *Jan is sleeping. I heard the dog barking.*

present perfect the form of the verb that combines the present of the **auxiliary verb** *have* with the **past participle**: *I have phoned for a taxi. Has Kim had lunch?*

present perfect continuous (or **progressive**) the form of the verb that combines the present of the **auxiliary verb** *have* with the **past participle** of *be* and the **present participle**: *It has been snowing; Have you been waiting long?*

present simple the form of the verb that has no **auxiliary verb** and in the third person singular takes **third person -s**: *They live in Houston. My back hurts.*

presentation the stage of a lesson where a new language item, such as a grammar structure, is introduced.

pre-teaching teaching language items in advance of the learners' needing to understand or use them, as in the pre-teaching of unfamiliar words before listening to a recording.

process writing an approach to the teaching of writing that emphasises the composing processes rather than the finished product.

productive skills the skills of speaking and writing, in contrast to the **receptive skills.**

progressive → **continuous**

project work the individual or collaborative production of a piece of work that usually involves some out-of-class research and preparation and which is then presented, in either spoken or written form or a combination of the two.

pronoun a word like *she, me, it, you* that can be used in place of a **noun** as **subject** or **object** of a sentence.

pronunciation the way the sounds of a language are spoken.

quantifier words or phrases which specify quantity or amount, e.g. *all, a few of, loads of.*

question tag a structure containing an **auxiliary verb** and a **pronoun**, which is added to a sentence to make a question, as in *It's a nice day, isn't it? You're not hungry, are you?*

rapport the feeling of mutual understanding and respect that exists between learners and their teacher.

realia real objects that are used in the classroom as **aids** for learning.

receptive skills the skills of listening and reading, in contrast to the **productive skills**.

reflexive pronoun a **pronoun** such as *myself, himself, themselves* used when the object of the verb refers to the same person as the subject: *I cut myself.*

register the way that the use of language varies according to variations in the context, such as the social distance between speakers or the topic or the medium.

regular verb a **verb** such as *work, live, start* whose past tense and **past participle** are formed by adding *-(e)d* to the **base form**: *worked, lived, started.* **Irregular verbs** do not follow this rule.

relative clause a **clause** that gives more information about something mentioned in the main clause: *This is the house where Freud lived.*

relative pronoun a **pronoun** that connects a **relative clause** to its noun: *This is the house where Freud lived.*

reported speech the way in which the sense of what someone has said (but not their exact wording) is incorporated into a text and where grammatical changes may be introduced: *'I'm hungry' = He said he was hungry.* Also called indirect speech, in contrast to direct speech.

reporting verb a verb like *say, tell, ask, wonder* that is typically used to report speech or thoughts.

rhythm the way that in speech some words are emphasised so as to give the effect of regular beats.

roleplay a classroom activity in which learners adopt different roles and act out a situation according to these roles.

routine any regularly used classroom procedure, such as checking attendance or reading a text aloud.

rubric the set of instructions for an exercise or a test that tells or shows the learners what they have to do.

scanning in reading, searching a text for specific information while ignoring other parts of the text, as when a reader searches a TV programme listing for the time of a news broadcast.

schema (plural **schemata**) the way that knowledge about a topic or a concept is represented and organised in the mind.

scheme of work the teacher's plan for a sequence of lessons.

self-access centre an area of a school that is equipped for learners to study independently, i.e. without teacher guidance.

self-assessment the process of learners evaluating their own learning progress.

sentence transformation an exercise type popular in exams, in which learners complete a sentence in such a way that its meaning is the same or similar to another sentence.

skill a way in which language is used, such as speaking or reading, in contrast to language systems, such as grammar and vocabulary.

skimming in reading, getting the main ideas or **gist**, of a text by reading it rapidly and without attention to detail.

stress the effect of emphasising certain syllables in speech; the stress pattern in individual words (**word stress**) is generally constant, but the stress in sentences (sentence stress) can vary according to what the speaker considers to be given, as opposed to new, information; the latter is typically stressed.

strong form the pronunciation of certain words, such as **auxiliary verbs** and **determiners**, when they are stressed, as in *Yes, I can* (/kæn/), which contrasts to their pronunciation when unstressed (called their **weak form**), e.g. *I can* (/kən/) *swim*.

structure any language pattern that generates specific instances; generally used to describe grammar items, such as verb forms.

subject the **noun phrase** that typically comes before the verb and tells you who or what is the agent or topic of the clause: *Chris caught the bus. The bus was crowded*.

subjective test → **objective test**

subskill a subcategory of one of the language **skills**; for example, inferencing is a subskill of the skill of reading.

substitution table a way of displaying, in the form of a grid, the way the different elements of a **structure** relate to one another.

suffix → **affix**

superlative the form of an adjective or adverb that is used to show an extreme or unique quality: *the fastest, the most unusual, the best*.

syllable a unit of pronunciation that is typically larger than a sound but smaller than a word; the word *syllable* has three syllables.

syllabus an item-by-item description of the teaching content of a course; a language syllabus is usually organised in terms of grammar **structures**.

synonym a word that has the same meaning as another one, as in *jail* and *prison*.

task a classroom activity whose focus is usually on communication, rather than on language practice for its own sake.

task-based learning a way of organising language learning around a syllabus of **tasks** rather than grammar **structures**.

teacher talking time (TTT) the extent to which the teacher dominates the speaking time in class.

teacher's book a guide for the teacher that usually accompanies most **coursebooks**.

tense the verb form which shows whether the speaker is referring to past, present or future.

In English, technically, there are only two tenses: present (*they go*) and past (*they went*).

test-teach-test a way of describing lessons that begin with some productive task which is followed by instruction that targets areas diagnosed as needing teaching, which is in turn followed by a repeat of the initial task or a similar task.

testing assessing learners' level or progress, either at the outset of a course (**placement testing**, diagnostic testing), during a course (**progress testing**) or at the end of a course (**achievement testing**).

text a continuous piece of spoken or written language

third person 's' the ending that is added to the base form of the verb in the present simple when talking about *he, she, it*, etc.: *she knows; Tom laughs*.

Total Physical Response a language teaching method in which learners respond to sequences of commands, based on the principle that language is best acquired through comprehension, not production.

transitive verb a verb, like *make, put, take*, that takes an **object**: *we made lunch*.

true/false questions comprehension-checking questions which require the learner to decide if a statement is true or false.

verb a word or words such as *worked, has, costs, takes off* that follows the **subject** of a **clause** and expresses what someone or something does or is.

verb pattern the sentence structure that is determined by the choice of **verb**. For example, the verb *make* can take the pattern verb + object + bare infinitive: *you made me do it*, whereas the verb *force* takes the pattern verb + object + *to*-infinitive: *you forced me to do it*.

visual aid a picture that is used for teaching purposes.

voice → **active, passive**

voiced sound a sound which is produced while the vocal cords are vibrating; some consonants, like *b, g, z*, are voiced, while others, like *p*, *k*, *s*, are unvoiced (or voiceless); all **vowels** are voiced.

vowel a sound that is produced without obstruction or constriction of the airflow from the lungs, as opposed to **consonants**, where the airflow is interrupted.

warmer, warm-up an activity done at the beginning of the lesson to ease the transition into the lesson itself.

weak form → **strong form**

wh-question a question that begins with a word like *what*, *when*, *why*, *how*, etc.

word order the way words and other elements are sequenced in **clauses** or sentences.

workbook a book of activities and exercises for homework or self-study that usually accompanies a **coursebook.**

***yes/no* question** a question that can be answered with either *yes* or *no*: *Are you married? Haven't you had lunch?*

zero article → **article**

Further reading list and useful websites

The learners and their contexts

How Languages are Learned (3rd edition), Patsy M. Lightbown and Nina Spada, Oxford University Press, 2006

Learner English (2nd edition), Michael Swan and Bernard Smith (eds), Cambridge University Press, 2001

Teaching Adult Second Language Learners, Heather McKay and Abigail Tom, Cambridge University Press, 1999

Classroom teaching

An A–Z of ELT, Scott Thornbury, Macmillan, 2006

How to Teach English (2nd edition), Jeremy Harmer, Pearson, 2007

How to Teach Grammar, Scott Thornbury, Pearson, 1999

How to Teach Speaking, Scott Thornbury, Pearson, 2005

How to Teach Vocabulary, Scott Thornbury, Pearson, 2002

How to Teach Writing, Jeremy Harmer, Pearson, 2004

Learning to Teach English, Peter Watkins, Delta Publishing, 2005

Learning Teaching (2nd edition), Jim Scrivener, Macmillan, 2005.

Planning Lessons and Courses, Tessa Woodward, Cambridge University Press, 2001

Practical English Language Teaching, David Nunan (ed), McGraw Hill, 2003

Teaching Listening Comprehension, Penny Ur Cambridge University Press, 1984

Teaching Reading Skills in a Foreign Language Christine Nuttall, Macmillan, 2005

Techniques and Principles in Language Teaching (2nd edition), Diane Larsen-Freeman, Oxford University Press, 2000

Language awareness

About Language: Tasks for Teachers of English, Scott Thornbury, Cambridge University Press, 1997

Cambridge Advanced Learner's Dictionary (2nd edition), Cambridge University Press, 2005

Grammar for English Language Teachers, Martin Parrott, Cambridge University Press, 2000

Practical English Usage (3rd edition), Michael Swan, Oxford University Press, 2005

Professional development

Professional Development for Language Teachers, Jack C. Richards and Thomas Farrell, Cambridge University Press, 2005

Useful websites

Resources

English Teaching Professional:
http://www.cambridge.org/elt/

Guardian Education: *TEFL*:
http://education.guardian.co.uk/tefl/

Humanising Language Teaching:
http://www.hltmag.co.uk/

It's Online:
http://www.its-online.com/

Onestop English:
http://www.onestopenglish.com/

Publishers

Cambridge University Press ELT:
http://www.cambridge.org/elt/

Oxford University Press ELT:
http://www.oup.com/elt/

Macmillan:
http://www.macmillanenglish.com/

Pearson Longman:
http://www.longman.com/teachers/

Delta Publishing:
http://www.deltapublishing.co.uk/

Other organisations

International Association of Teachers of English as a Foreign Language (*IATEFL*):
http://www.iatefl.org/

Teachers of English to Speakers of Other Languages (*TESOL*): http://www.tesol.org/

Cambridge ESOL: http://www.cambridgeesol.org/

British Council: http://www.britishcouncil.org/

Study English Australia (*ELICOS*):
http://www.elicos.com/

Acknowledgements

We would like to thank Nóirín Burke, Roslyn Henderson and Frances Amrani at Cambridge University Press for all their support, guidance and encouragement.

Our thanks are also due to Jill Florent and Penny Hands for their editorial expertise and to all those who commented on drafts of the manuscript, particularly Norman Cain, Jim Chapman, Lindsay Clandfield, Fay Drewry, Isobel Drury, Leona Maslova, Steven McGuire, Gabi Megyesi, David Noble, Mary O'Leary, David Riddell, Lisa Sanderson, Sandra Stevens, Craig Thaine, Sandee Thompson, Liz Walter and Frances Watkins.

We are also indebted to the Teaching Awards team at Cambridge ESOL, particularly Monica Poulter and Clare Harrison, for helpful suggestions and comments throughout the project.

The authors and publishers acknowledge the following sources of copyright material and are grateful for the permissions granted. While every effort has been made, it has not always been possible to identify the sources of all the material used, or to trace all copyright holders. If any omissions are brought to our notice, we will be happy to include the appropriate acknowledgements on reprinting.

p. 10: Helbling Languages for text 'Multiple Intelligences in EFL' by Herbert Puchta and Mario Rinvolucri. © Helbling Languages 2005;

p. 11: 'Olga and Miguel Learning – Tips' from *Over to us! (3rd ESO) Student's Book* by Palencia and Thornbury. Published by Longman, 1997. Illustration © El Pais, Madrid, Spain;

p. 11: Pearson Education for the text 'Using a dictionary' from *The Beginners' Choice Student's Book,* by Mohamed and Acklam. Published by Longman, 1992, p. 49 'Skills, Reading' from *Elementary Matters* by Bell and Gower. Published by Longman, 1997, p. 94 transcript from *The Intermediate Choice Student's Book,* by Mohamed and Acklam. Published by Longman, 1995, p. 109 'Do you remember?' And p. 168 'Say and tell' from *Cutting Edge Intermediate Student's Book,* by Moor and Cunningham. Published by Longman, 1998, p. 126 text from *Cutting Edge (Intermediate)* by Cunningham and Moor. Published by Longman, 1998, p. 127 text from *The Intermediate Choice* by Mohamed and Acklam. Published by Longman, 1995, p. 134 'Language focus 2' from *Cutting Edge Pre-Intermediate Student's Book* by Cunningham and Moor. Published by Longman, 2005, p. 141 'Conditional Sentences' from *Longman English Grammar* by Alexander. Published by Longman, 1988, p. 152 'Writing' from *The Intermediate Choice Student's Book,* by Mohamed and Acklam. Published by Longman, 1995, p. 163 text from *The Pronunciation Book* by Bowen and Marks. Published by Longman, 1992, p. 172 'Writing: connecting ideas' from *The Intermediate Choice Workbook* by Thornbury. Published by Longman, 1995. Used with permission of Pearson Education Limited;

p. 12: Cambridge University Press for the text 'Learning tip' from *Touchstone 1 Student's Book,* by McCarthy, McCarten, Sandiford. Copyright © 2005, p. 20 dictionary entries from *Cambridge Advanced Learner's Dictionary.* Copyright © 2003, p. 44 'listening lesson', p. 45 text, p. 117 'Get ready… get it right' from *face2face Pre-Intermediate Student's Book,* by Redston and Cunningham. Copyright © 2005, p. 77 'Board Game' from *Grammar Games,* by Rinvolucri. Copyright © 1985, p. 99 'The words you need to talk about change' from *English365 2 Student's Book,* by Dignen, Flinders and Sweeney. Copyright © 2004, p. 126 text from English Grammar in Use, by Murphy. Copyright © 1985, p.135 text and p. 151 'Building language' from *Touchstone Student's Book 2,* by McCarthy, McCarten, Sandiford. Copyright © 2005, p. 139 'Mistakes' from *Language in Use Upper Intermediate Classroom book,* by Doff and Jones. Copyright © 1997, p. 142 text from *New Cambridge English Course 4 Student's Book,* by Swan, Walter, O'Sullivan. Copyright © 1993, p. 159 text from *New Cambridge English Course 3 Student's Book,* by Swan, Walter, O'Sullivan. Copyright © 1992, p. 172 text from *Business Explorer 2 Student's Book,* by Knight and O'Neil. Copyright © 2002. Reproduced by permission of Cambridge University Press;

p. 31 and p. 140: Oxford University Press for text from *New Headway Intermediate Student's Book,* by Soars and Soars. Copyright © 1996, p. 53 and p. 152 text from *Headway Pre Intermediate Student's Book,* by Soars and Soars. Copyright © 1991, p. 63 'a formal email' from *New English File Pre-Intermediate Student's Book,* by Oxenden, Latham-Koenig and Seligson. Copyright © 2005, p. 67 and p. 68 text from *Project*

English, by Hutchinson. Copyright © 1986, p. 71 text from *How English Works,* by Swan and Walter. Copyright © 1997, pp. 86–87 'Motivation in the classroom setting' from *How Languages are Learned,* by Lightbown and Spada. Copyright © 1999, p. 93 text from *Clockwise Elementary Student's Book,* by Potten and Potten. Copyright © 2001, p. 93 text from *Clockwise Advanced Student's Book,* by Jeffries. Copyright © 2001, p. 139 'speaking it's your turn!' from *Natural English Pre Intermediate,* by Gairns and Redman. Copyright © 2005, p. 140 text from *Clockwise Intermediate,* by Forsyth. Copyright © 2000, pp. 164–165 'Useful language' from *Clockwise Pre-Intermediate Classbook,* by McGowen and Richardson. Copyright © 2000, p. 168 'affixes' from *Natural English Upper Intermediate Student's Book* by Gairns and Redman Copyright © 2003. Reproduced by permission of Oxford University Press. Copyright © Oxford University Press;

p. 48: text from www.gxangalo.com;

p. 54: TNT Magazine for 'Backpacker Q&A' by Jennifer Arnott, from *TNT Magazine,* 5 June 2006. Used by permission of TNT Magazine. www.tntmagazine.com;

p. 54: Ananova for the text 'Transports of Delight' from a web article 5 May 2006 and for p. 66 text 'Aliens will chat to us in 20 years' from a web article 30 March 2006. Used by permission of Ananova. www.ananova.com;

p. 55: Russell Grant Astrology Ltd for the Star signs from the Russell Grant horoscope website. Used by permission of Russell Grant Astrology Ltd. www.russellgrant.com;

p. 76: Mirrorpix/DailyMirror for the newspaper article and photograph 'Boat Ordeal Britons Survive on seaweed!' 14 August 1988 © Mirrorpix/DailyMirror;

p. 77: Thomson Learning for 'Speaking' and p. 96 text from *Innovations Pre-Intermediate, A Course in Natural English 1st edition* by Dellar/Hocking/Walkley. © 2004. Reprinted with permission from Heinle. A division of Thomson Learning: www.thomsonrights.com;

p. 95, pp. 132–133 and p. 151: Macmillan Education for text from *Inside Out Upper Intermediate Student's Book.* © Sue Kay and Vaughn Jones 2001, p. 101 text from *An A–Z of ELT.* © Scott Thornbury 2006, p. 111 table from *Learning Teaching.* © Jim Scrivener 2005, p. 156 'The phonemic chart' from *Sound Foundations.* © Adrian Underhill 1994. Reproduced by permission of Macmillan Publishers Ltd;

p. 98: United States Coastguard for text from USCG Safety Manual, Vol II. Copyright © United States Coastguard;

p. 100: Council of Europe for adapted text from *A Common European Framework of Reference for Languages: Learning, Teaching, Assessment.* Copyright © Council of Europe;

pp. 104–105: NSW Adult Migrant English Service for 'Writing a formal letter of complaint' from *Beach Street Intermediate Student Book 2,* by Susan Delaruelle. Copyright © 1998. Used by permission of NSW AMES;

p. 112: Fiona Joseph for text from *How to Teach an FCE class.* Copyright Flo-Joe 2003. Used by permission of Fiona Joseph;

p. 118: Becta for text 'Interactive Whiteboards' from a web article *What the research says.* Used by permission of Becta. www.becta.org;

p. 119: extract from *Teacher* by Sylvia Ashton-Warner. Published by Penguin Books 1966;

p. 124: Woman's Weekly for the article 'We changed our lives, you could too' by Frances Quinn, *Woman's Weekly,* 10 January 2006. Article supplied courtesy of Woman's Weekly;

p. 130: Geoff Dyer for the extract from *White Sands.* Copyright Geoff Dyer. Originally published in *Granta 91* (Autumn 2005). Used by permission of Geoff Dyer;

p. 149 and p. 153: Delta Publishing for the text from *Learning to Teach English,* by Watkins © Delta Publishing. Used by permission of Delta Publishing;

p. 166: Men's Health Magazine for 'Step Class' from *Men's Health,* April 1996. Used by permission of Men's Health Magazine;

pp. 171–173: Kingfisher Books for dictionary entries adapted from *Pocket Encyclopedia* by A Jack. Published by Kingfisher Books.

The publishers are also grateful to the following for permission to reproduce copyright photographs and material:

pp. 36: Alamy Images/©FAN Travelstock for photograph of Eiffel Tower; ©K-Photos for photograph of Sydney Opera House; ©Robert Harding for photograph of Taj Mahal; ©Visions of America, LLC for photograph of Manhattan Skyline; Getty Images for photograph of Pyramids; ©Brand X for photograph of Great Wall of China and ©Digital Vision for photograph of Big Ben;

pp. 92: Getty Images for photograph on the left; Punchstock ©Bananastock for photograph on the right;

Picture Research by Hilary Luckcock.